PAPER BACK LYRICS

COMPLETE
OVER 185 SONGS

Christmas

HAL•LEONARD®

ISBN-13: 978-1-4234-1191-8
ISBN-10: 1-4234-1191-9

For all works contained herein:
Unauthorized copying, arranging, adapting, recording or public
performance is an infringement of copyright.
Infringers are liable under the law.

HAL•LEONARD®
CORPORATION

7777 W. BLUEMOUND RD. P.O. BOX 13819 MILWAUKEE, WI 53213

Visit Hal Leonard Online at
www.halleonard.com

CONTENTS

A Caroling We Go

Music and Lyrics by Johnny Marks

A caroling, a caroling, a caroling we go,
Hearts filled with music and cheeks aglow.
From house to house we bring the message of the King again,
Peace on Earth, goodwill to men,
Peace on Earth, goodwill to men.

We bring you season's greetings and we wish the best to you,
And may our wish last the whole year through.
Come join us if you will as we are singing once again,
Peace on Earth, goodwill to men,
Peace on Earth, goodwill to men.

Now you may have your holly and perhaps some mistletoe,
Maybe a fir tree and maybe snow.
But wouldn't it be wonderful if we could have again,
Peace on Earth, goodwill to men,
Peace on Earth, goodwill to men.

Repeat Verse 1

Copyright © 1966 (Renewed 1994) St. Nicholas Music Inc., 1619 Broadway, New York, New York 10019
All Rights Reserved

Almost Day

Words and Music by Huddie Ledbetter

Chickens a-crowin' for midnight, it's almost day;
Chickens a-crowin' for midnight, it's almost day.
Candy canes and sugar plums, on Christmas Day;
Candy canes and sugar plums, on Christmas Day.

Mama'll stuff a turkey on Christmas Day;
Mama'll stuff a turkey on Christmas Day.
Santa Claus is coming on Christmas Day;
Santa Claus is coming on Christmas Day.

TRO - © Copyright 1952 (Renewed) Folkways Music Publishers, Inc., New York, NY
International Copyright Secured
All Rights Reserved Including Public Performance For Profit
Used by Permission

All I Want for Christmas Is You

Words and Music by Mariah Carey and Walter Afanasieff

I don't want a lot for Christmas,
There is just one thing I need.
I don't care about the presents
Underneath the Christmas tree.

I just want you for my own,
More than you could ever know.
Make my wish come true:
All I want for Christmas is you, yeah.

I don't want a lot for Christmas,
There is just one thing I need
And I don't care about the presents,
Underneath the Christmas tree.

I don't need to hand my stocking
There upon the fireplace.
Santa Claus won't make me happy
With a toy on Christmas day.

I just want you for my own,
More than you could ever know.
Make my wish come true:
All I want for Christmas is you. You, baby.

I won't ask for much this Christmas,
I won't even wish for snow.
And I, I'm just gonna keep on waiting
Underneath the mistletoe.

Copyright © 1994 Sony/ATV Tunes LLC, Wallyworld Music and Rye Songs
All Rights for Sony/ATV Tunes LLC and Wallyworld Music Administered by Sony/ATV Music Publishing,
    8 Music Square West, Nashville, TN 37203
All Rights for Rye Songs Administered by Songs of Universal, Inc.
International Copyright Secured   All Rights Reserved

I won't make a list and send it
To the North Pole for Saint Nick.
I won't even stay awake
To hear those magic reindeer click.

I just want you here tonight,
Holding on to me so tight.
What more can I do?
Baby all I want for Christmas is you. You, baby.

Oh, all the lights are shining so brightly everywhere,
And the sound of children's laughter fills the air,
And everyone is singing,
I hear those sleighbells ringing.
Santa won't you please
Bring me what I really need,
Won't you please bring my baby to me?

Oh, I don't want a lot for Christmas,
This is all I'm asking for.
I just want to see my baby
Standing right outside my door.

I just want him for my own,
More than you could ever know.
Make my wish come true:
All I want for Christmas is you.
Ooh, baby, all I want for Christmas is you baby.

Repeat and Fade:
All I want for Christmas is you, baby.

Angels from the Realms of Glory

Words by James Montgomery
Music by Henry T. Smart

Angels from the realms of glory,
Wing your flight o'er all the earth;
Ye who sang creation's story,
Now proclaim Messiah's birth.

Refrain:
Come and worship!
Come and worship!
Worship Christ the newborn King!

Shepherds in the fields abiding,
Watching o'er your flocks by night,
God with man is now residing;
Yonder shines the infant Light.
Refrain

Sages, leave your contemplations,
Brighter visions beam afar,
Seek the great Desire of nations,
Ye have seen His natal star.
Refrain

Saints before the altar bending,
Watching long in hope and fear,
Suddenly the Lord, descending,
In His temple shall appear.

Refrain

Copyright © 2002 by HAL LEONARD CORPORATION
International Copyright Secured   All Rights Reserved

Angels We Have Heard on High

Traditional French Carol
Translated by James Chadwick

Angels we have heard on high,
Singing sweetly o'er the plains,
And the mountains in reply
Echoing their joyous strains.
Gloria in excelsis Deo,
Gloria in excelsis Deo.

Shepherds, why this jubilee?
Why your joyous strains prolong?
What the gladsome tidings be
Which inspire your heavenly song?
Gloria in excelsis Deo,
Gloria in excelsis Deo.

Come to Bethlehem and see
Him whose birth the angels sing.
Come adore on bended knee
Christ the Lord, the newborn King.
Gloria in excelsis Deo,
Gloria in excelsis Deo.

See within a manger laid
Jesus, Lord of heav'n and earth!
Mary, Joseph, lend your aid;
With us sing our Savior's birth.
Gloria in excelsis Deo,
Gloria in excelsis Deo.

Copyright © 2002 by HAL LEONARD CORPORATION
International Copyright Secured   All Rights Reserved

As Long as There's Christmas

Music by Rachel Portman
Lyrics by Don Black

from Walt Disney's *Beauty and the Beast - The Enchanted Christmas*

Female:
There is more to this time of year
Than sleighbells and holly,

Male:
Misteltoe and snow.

Both:
Those things will come and go.

Female:
Don't look inside a stocking.
Don't look under the tree.
The one thing we're looking for
Is something we can't see.

Male:
Far more precious than silver
And more splendid than gold,
This is something to treasure,
But it's something we can't hold.

© 1997 Wonderland Music Company, Inc.
All Rights Reserved   Used by Permission

Both:
As long as there's Christmas, I truly believe

Male:
That hope is the greatest

Both:
Of the gifts we'll receive,

Male:
We'll receive.
As we all pray together, it's a time to rejoice.

Female:
And though we may look diff'rent,

Both:
We'll all sing with one voice.

Male:
Whoa.

Both:
As long as there's Christmas,
I truly believe
That hope is the greatest of the gifts we'll receive.
As long as there's Christmas, we'll all be just fine.
A star shines above us,

Female:
Lighting your way

Male:
And mine.

Female:
Oh.

Male:
Light my way.

Female:
You know I will.

Both:
As long as there's Christmas,
I truly believe
That hope is the greatest of the gifts we'll receive.
As long as our guiding star shines above,
There'll always be Christmas,

Male:
So there always will be a time

Both:
When the world is filled with peace and love.

As with Gladness Men of Old

Words by William Chatterton Dix
Music by Conrad Kocher

As with gladness men of old
Did the guiding star behold;
As with joy they hailed its light,
Leading onward, beaming bright;
So, most gracious Lord, may we
Evermore be led to Thee.

As with joyful steps they sped
To that lowly manger bed,
There to bend the knee before
Him whom heav'n and earth adore;
So may we with willing feet
Ever seek thy mercy seat.

As they offered gifts most rare
At that manger rude and bare;
So may we with holy joy,
Pure and free from sin's alloy,
All our costliest treasures bring,
Christ, to Thee, our heav'nly King.

Holy Jesus, ev'ry day
Keep us in the narrow way;
And when earthly things are past,
Bring our ransomed souls at last
Where they need no star to guide,
Where no clouds Thy glory hide.

Copyright © 2002 by HAL LEONARD CORPORATION
International Copyright Secured   All Rights Reserved

Auld Lang Syne

Words by Robert Burns
Traditional Scottish Melody

Should auld acquaintance be forgot,
And never brought to mind?
Should auld acquaintance be forgot
And days of Auld Lang Syne?

For Auld Lang Syne, my dear,
For Auld Lang Syne,
We'll take a cup of kindness yet
For Auld Lang Syne.

Copyright © 2002 by HAL LEONARD CORPORATION
International Copyright Secured   All Rights Reserved

Away in a Manger

Traditional
Words by John T. McFarland (v.3)
Music by James R. Murray

Away in a manger, no crib for His bed,
The little Lord Jesus lay down His sweet head;
The stars in the bright sky looked down where he lay,
The little Lord Jesus, asleep in the hay.

The cattle are lowing, the baby awakes,
But little Lord Jesus no crying he makes.
I love Thee, Lord Jesus! Look down from the sky,
And stay by my side until morning is nigh.

Be near me, Lord Jesus; I ask Thee to stay
Close by me forever, and love me, I pray.
Bless all the dear children in Thy tender care,
And take us to heaven, to live with Thee there.

Copyright © 2002 by HAL LEONARD CORPORATION
International Copyright Secured   All Rights Reserved

Baby, It's Cold Outside

By Frank Loesser

from the Motion Picture *Neptune's Daughter*

Note: The song is a duet; the male lines are in parentheses.

I really can't stay,
(But baby it's cold outside!)
I've got to go 'way.
(But baby it's cold outside!)
This evening has been
(Been hoping that you'd drop in!)
So very nice.
(I'll hold your hands they're just like ice.)
My mother will start to worry
(Beautiful, what's your hurry?)
And father will be pacing the floor.
(Listen to the fireplace roar!)
So really I'd better scurry,
(Beautiful, please don't hurry.)
Well, maybe just half a drink more.
(Put some records on while I pour.)
The neighbors might think
(But, baby it's bad out there.)
Say, what's in the drink?
(No cabs to be had out there.)
I wish I knew how
(Your eyes are like starlight now)
To break the spell.
(I'll take your hat your hair looks swell.)
I ought to say "No, no, no, Sir!"
(Mind if I move in closer?)
At least I'm gonna say that I tried.
(What's the sense of hurting my pride.)

© 1948 (Renewed) FRANK MUSIC CORP.
All Rights Reserved

I really can't stay
(Oh, baby, don't hold out,)
Ah, but it's cold outside.
(Baby, it's cold outside.)

I simply must go.
(But baby it's cold outside!)
The answer is no!
(But baby it's cold outside!)
The welcome has been,
(How lucky that you dropped in!)
So nice and warm.
(Look out the window at that storm.)
My sister will be suspicious,
(Gosh, your lips look delicious.)
My brother will be there at the door.
(Waves upon a tropical shore!)
My maiden aunt's mind is vicious.
(Gosh, your lips are delicious)
Well, maybe just a cigarette more.
(Never such a blizzard before.)
I've got to get home
(But, baby, you'd freeze out there)
Say, lend me a comb.
(It's up to your knees out there.)
You've really been grand,
(I thrill when you touch my hand)
But don't you see.
(How can you do this thing to me.)
There's bound to be talk tomorrow.
(Think of my life-long sorrow.)
At least there will be plenty implied.
(If you caught pneumonia and died.)
I really can't stay
(Get over that old doubt,)
Ah, but it's cold outside.
(Baby, it's cold outside.)

Because It's Christmas
(For All the Children)

Music by Barry Manilow
Lyric by Bruce Sussman and Jack Feldman

Tonight the stars shine for the children.
And light the way for dreams to fly.
Tonight our love comes wrapped in ribbons.
The world is right and hopes are high.
And from a dark and frosted window
A child appears to search the sky
Because it's Christmas, because it's Christmas.

Tonight belongs to all the children.
Tonight the joy rings through the air.
And so, we send our tender blessings
To all the children everywhere,
To see the smiles and hear the laughter;
A time to give, a time to share,
Because it's Christmas for now and forever
For all the children and for the children in us all.

Repeat Verse 2

Copyright © 1986 by Careers-BMG Music Publishing, Appoggiatura Music and Camp Songs Music
All Rights Administered by Careers-BMG Music Publishing
International Copyright Secured   All Rights Reserved

Blue Christmas

Words and Music by Billy Hayes and Jay Johnson

I'll have a blue Christmas, without you.
I'll be so blue thinking about you.
Decorations of red on a green Christmas tree
Won't mean a thing if you're not here with me.

I'll have a blue Christmas, that's certain.
And when that blue heartache starts hurtin',
You'll be doin' all right, with your Christmas of white,
But I'll have a blue, blue Christmas.

Copyright © 1948 UNIVERSAL - POLYGRAM INTERNATIONAL PUBLISHING, INC.
Copyright Renewed
All Rights Reserved   Used by Permission

Bring a Torch, Jeannette, Isabella

17th Century French Provençal Carol

Bring a torch, Jeannette, Isabella,
Bring a torch, come swiftly and run.
Christ is born, tell the folk of the village,
Jesus is sleeping in His cradle,
Ah, ah, beautiful is the Mother,
Ah, ah, beautiful is her Son.

Hasten now, good folk of the village,
Hasten now, the Christ Child to see.
You will find him asleep in a manger,
Quietly come and whisper softly,
Hush, hush, peacefully now He slumbers,
Hush, hush, peacefully now He sleeps.

Copyright © 2002 by HAL LEONARD CORPORATION
International Copyright Secured   All Rights Reserved

Burgundian Carol

Words and Music by Oscar Brand

The winter season of the year,
When to the world our Lord was born,
The ox and donkey, so they say,
Did keep His Holy Presence warm.
How many oxen and donkeys now,
If they were there when first He came,
How many oxen and donkeys you know
At such a time would do the same?

As soon as to these humble beasts
Appeared our Lord, so mild and sweet,
With joy they knelt before His grace,
And gently kissed His tiny feet.
If we, like oxen and donkeys then,
In spite of all the things we've heard,
Would be like oxen and donkeys then,
We'd hear the truth, believe His word.

TRO - © Copyright 1951 (Renewed) and 1952 (Renewed) Folkways Music Publishers, Inc., New York, NY
International Copyright Secured
All Rights Reserved Including Public Performance For Profit
Used by Permission

C-H-R-I-S-T-M-A-S

Words by Jenny Lou Carson
Music by Eddy Arnold

When I was but a youngster Christmas meant one thing:
That I'd be getting lots of toys that day.
I learned a whole lot diff'rent when mother sat me down
And taught me to spell Christmas this way.

C is for the Christ child born upon this day,
H for herald angels in the night.
R means our Redeemer,
I means Israel,
S is for the star that shone so bright.
T is for three wise men, they who traveled far,
M is for the manger where He lay.
A's for all He stands for,
S means shepherds came,
And that's why there's a Christmas day.

Copyright © 1949 by Hill & Range Songs, Inc.
Copyright Renewed
All Rights Administered by Unichappell Music Inc.
International Copyright Secured   All Rights Reserved

Carol of the Bells

Ukrainian Christmas Carol

Hark to the bells, hark to the bells,
Telling us all Jesus is King!

Strongly they chime, sound with a rhyme,
Christmas is here, welcome the King!

Hark to the bells, hark to the bells,
This is the day, day of the King!

Peal out the news o'er hill and dale,
And 'round the town telling the tale.

Hark to the bells, hark to the bells,
Telling us all Jesus is King!

Come, one and all happily sing
Songs of good will, O let them sing!

Ring, silv'ry bells,
Sing, joyous bells!

Strongly they chime, sound with a rhyme,
Christmas is here, welcome the King!

Hark to the bells, hark to the bells,
Telling us all Jesus is King!

Ring! Ring! bells.

Copyright © 2006 by HAL LEONARD CORPORATION
International Copyright Secured   All Rights Reserved

Caroling, Caroling

Words by Wihla Hutson
Music by Alfred Burt

Caroling, caroling, now we go,
Christmas bells are ringing!
Caroling, caroling through the snow,
Christmas bells are ringing!
Joyous voices sweet and clear,
Sing the sad of heart to cheer.
Ding, dong, ding, dong,
Christmas bells are ringing!

Caroling, caroling through the town,
Christmas bells are ringing!
Caroling, caroling up and down,
Christmas bells are ringing!
Mark ye well the song we sing,
Gladsome tidings now we bring.
Ding, dong, ding, dong,
Christmas bells are ringing!

Caroling, caroling, near and far,
Christmas bells are ringing!
Following, following yonder star,
Christmas bells are ringing!
Sing we all this happy morn,
"Lo, the King of heav'n is born!"
Ding, dong, ding, dong,
Christmas bells are ringing!

TRO - © Copyright 1954 (Renewed) and 1957 (Renewed) Hollis Music, Inc., New York, NY
International Copyright Secured
All Rights Reserved Including Public Performance For Profit
Used by Permission

The Chipmunk Song

Words and Music by Ross Bagdasarian

Christmas, Christmas time is near,
Time for toys and time for cheer.
We've been good but we can't last,
Hurry Christmas, hurry fast!
Want a plane that loops the loop;
Me, I want a hula hoop.
We can hardly stand the wait,
Please, Christmas, don't be late.

Copyright © 1958 Bagdasarian Productions LLC
All Rights Controlled and Administered by Bagdasarian Productions LLC
All Rights Reserved   Used by Permission

Christ Was Born on Christmas Day

Traditional

Christ was born on Christmas Day,
Wreath the holly, twine the bay;
Christus natus hodie;
The Babe, the Son, the Holy One of Mary.

He is born to set us free,
He is born our Lord to be,
Ex Maria Virgine;
The God, the Lord, by all adored forever.

Let the bright red berries glow,
Everywhere in goodly show;
Christus natus hodie;
The Babe, the Son, the Holy One of Mary.

Christian men, rejoice and sing,
'Tis the birthday of a king,
Ex Maria Virgine;
The God, the Lord, by all adored forever.

Copyright © 2006 by HAL LEONARD CORPORATION
International Copyright Secured   All Rights Reserved

A Christmas Carol

Words and Music by Leslie Bricusse

from *Scrooge*

Sing a song of gladness and cheer
For the time of Christmas is here.
Look around about you and see
What a world of wonder this world can be.

Sing a Christmas carol, sing a Christmas carol,
Sing a Christmas carol like the children do
And enjoy the beauty, all the joy and beauty
That a merry Christmas can bring to you.

Copyright © 1970; Renewed 1998 Stage And Screen Music, Ltd. (BMI)
Worldwide Rights for Stage And Screen Music, Ltd. Administered by Cherry River Music Co.
International Copyright Secured   All Rights Reserved

Christmas Is

Lyrics by Spence Maxwell
Music by Percy Faith

Christmas is sleighbells, Christmas is sharing,
Christmas is holly, Christmas is caring.

Christmas is children who just can't go to sleep;
Christmas is memories, the kind you always keep.

Deck the halls and give a cheer
For all the things that Christmas is each year.

Christmas, Merry Christmas,
When all your wishes come true.

Christmas is carols to warm you in the snow;
Christmas is bedtime where no one wants to go.

All the world is tinsel bright
So glad to know that Christmas is tonight.

Christmas, Merry Christmas,
When all your wishes come true.

Christmas, Merry Christmas,
May all your wishes come true.

Copyright © 1966 UNIVERSAL - POLYGRAM INTERNATIONAL PUBLISHING, INC.
Copyright Renewed
All Rights Reserved   Used by Permission

Christmas Is A-Comin'
(May God Bless You)

Words and Music by Frank Luther

When I'm feelin' blue, an' when I'm feelin' low,
Then I start to think about the happiest man I know;
He doesn't mind the snow an' he doesn't mind the rain,
But all December you will hear him at your windowpane,
A-singin' again an' again an' again an' again an' again an' again.

Christmas is a-comin' and the geese are getting' fat,
Please to put a penny in a poor man's hat.
If you haven't got a penny, a ha' penny'll do,
If you haven't got a ha' penny, may God bless you.
God bless you, gentlemen, God bless you,
If you haven't got a ha' penny, may God bless you.

Christmas is a-comin' and the lights are on the tree,
How about a turkey leg for poor old me?
If you haven't got a turkey leg, a turkey wing'll do,
If you haven't got a turkey wing, may God bless you.
God bless you, gentlemen, God bless you,
If you haven't got a turkey wing, may God bless you.

Christmas is a-comin' and the egg is in the nog,
Please to let me sit around your old yule log.
If you'd rather I didn't sit around, to stand around'll do,
If you'd rather I didn't stand around, may God bless you.
God bless you, gentlemen, God bless you,
If you'd rather I didn't stand around, may God bless you.
If you haven't got a thing for me, may God bless you.

© 1953, 1956 (Renewed) FRANK MUSIC CORP.
All Rights Reserved

Christmas Is Just About Here

Words and Music by Loonis McGlohon

It's fun hanging 'round in the kitchen,
Where everything smells so nice;
Oh, Mama is a baking a fruitcake
With apples, honey, and spice.
The children are getting excited
Whenever gray clouds appear;
The almanac promised a snowfall,
And Christmas is just about here.

'Tis the season to be jolly,
Everybody feels young.
Deck the halls with boughs of holly
And let the stockings be hung.
We'll soon have a visit from Saint Nick,
And maybe he'll bring reindeer.
We never outgrow the warm feeling
When Christmas is just about here.

Everybody has a list of things to do.
Buy a tie for Dad which will look good with blue.
Did you mail Aunt Mary a Christmas card?
Tie a ribbon on the lamppost out in the yard.

TRO - © Copyright 1984 and 1985 Melody Trails, Inc., New York, NY
International Copyright Secured
All Rights Reserved Including Public Performance For Profit
Used by Permission

It's great fun when Papa will take us
To pick out a Christmas tree;
Mom says to be sure that we choose one
That's big and taller than me.
It's time to start wrapping the presents
For everyone we hold dear,
Then hiding them back in the closet,
'Cause Christmas is just about here.

Deck the halls with boughs of holly,
Fill up the candy jar.
Light a candle in the window
And hang up the Christmas star.
I like everything about Christmas,
The holly and holiday cheer.
Let's hurry up and get ready,
'Cause Christmas is just about here.

The Christmas Song (Chestnuts Roasting on an Open Fire)

Music and Lyric by Mel Torme and Robert Wells

Chestnuts roasting on an open fire,
Jack Frost nipping at your nose,
Yuletide carols being sung by a choir,
And folks dressed up like Eskimos.

Everybody knows a turkey and some mistletoe
Help to make the season bright.
Tiny tots with their eyes all aglow
Will find it hard to sleep tonight.

They know that Santa's on his way;
He's loaded lots of toys and goodies on his sleigh,
And every mother's child is gonna spy
To see if reindeer really know how to fly.

And so I'm offering this simple phrase
To kids from one to ninety-two.
Although it's been said many times, many ways,
"Merry Christmas to you."

© 1946 (Renewed) EDWIN H. MORRIS & COMPANY, A Division of MPL Music Publishing, Inc. and
    SONY/ATV TUNES LLC
All Rights on behalf of SONY/ATV TUNES LLC Administered by SONY/ATV MUSIC PUBLISHING,
    8 Music Square West, Nashville, TN 37203
All Rights Reserved

Christmas Time Is Here

Words by Lee Mendelson
Music by Vince Guaraldi

from the television special *A Charlie Brown Christmas*

Christmas time is here,
Happiness and cheer.
Fun for all that children call
Their favorite time of year.

Snowflakes in the air,
Carols everywhere.
Olden times and ancient rhymes
Of love and dreams to share.

Refrain:
Sleigh bells in the air,
Beauty everywhere.
Yuletide by the fireside
And joyful memories there.
Christmas time is here,
We'll be drawing near.
Oh, that we could always see
Such spirit through the year.

Repeat Refrain

Copyright © 1966 LEE MENDELSON FILM PRODUCTIONS, INC.
Copyright Renewed
International Copyright Secured   All Rights Reserved

The Christmas Waltz

Words by Sammy Cahn
Music by Jule Styne

Frosted window panes,
Candles gleaming inside,
Painted candy canes on the tree;
Santa's on his way,
He's filled his sleigh with things,
Things for you and for me.

It's the time of year
When the world falls in love,
Every song you hear seems to say:
"Merry Christmas,
May your New Year dreams come true."
And this song of mine,
In three-quarter time,
Wishes you and yours
The same thing too.

Copyright © 1954 by Producers Music Publishing Co. and Cahn Music Company
Copyright Renewed
All Rights for Producers Music Publishing Co. Administered by Chappell & Co.
All Rights for Cahn Music Company Administered by WB Music Corp.
International Copyright Secured   All Rights Reserved

Cold December Nights

Words and Music by Michael McCary and Shawn Stockman

Cold December nights like this make me really scared.
You're not really there and my tree is really bare.
Another lonely night, no gifts, no toys underneath my tree.
Can this really be?
I'm singing Christmas carols
And there's no Christmas for me?

Refrain:
Why aren't you next to me
Celebrating Christmas?
Why can't you see what hurts so bad?
How can you go
Without paying mind to my sorrow
On this cold December night?

Ooh, the stars shine bright as the night air,
And the thought of you not being here makes me shed a tear.
And yet matters remain unclear about why you're gone,
Or if you'll ever return to this broken heart.
Life is so torn apart and God knows,
God knows where I need to start rebuilding.

Refrain

Copyright © 1993 by Black Panther Publishing Co., Slim Shot Publishing and Ensign Music LLC
International Copyright Secured   All Rights Reserved

Come, Thou Long-Expected Jesus

Words by Charles Wesley
Music adapted by Henry J. Gauntlett

Come, Thou long-expected Jesus,
Born to set Thy people free.
From our fears and sins release us;
Let us find our rest in Thee.
Israel's strength and consolation,
Hope of all the earth Thou art;
Dear desire of ev'ry nation,
Joy of ev'ry longing heart.

Born Thy people to deliver,
Born a child and yet a king,
Born to reign in us forever,
Now Thy gracious kingdom bring.
By Thine own eternal Spirit
Rule in all our hearts alone.
By Thine all sufficient merit,
Raise us to Thy glorious throne.

Copyright © 2002 by HAL LEONARD CORPORATION
International Copyright Secured   All Rights Reserved

The Coventry Carol

Traditional

Lullay, thou little tiny child,
By by, lully lullay.
Lullay, thou little tiny child,
By by, lully lullay.

O sisters too, how may we do,
For to preserve this day.
This poor youngling for whom we sing,
By by, lully lullay.

Herod the king, in his raging,
Charged he hath this day.
His men of might, in his own sight,
All young children to slay.

That woe is me, poor child for thee!
And ever morn and day,
For thy parting nor say nor sing,
By by, lully lullay.

Copyright © 2002 by HAL LEONARD CORPORATION
International Copyright Secured   All Rights Reserved

Deck the Hall

Traditional Welsh Carol

Deck the hall with boughs of holly,
Fa la la la la, la la la la.
'Tis the season to be jolly,
Fa la la la la, la la la la.
Don we now our gay apparel,
Fa la la, la la la, la la la.
Troll the ancient Yuletide carol,
Fa la la la la, la la la la.

See the blazing yule before us,
Fa la la la la, la la la la.
Strike the harp and join the chorus,
Fa la la la la, la la la la.
Follow me in merry measure,
Fa la la, la la la, la la la.
While I tell of Yuletide treasure,
Fa la la la la, la la la la.

Fast away the old year passes,
Fa la la la la, la la la la.
Hail the new, ye lads and lasses,
Fa la la la la, la la la la.
Sing we joyous, all together,
Fa la la, la la la, la la la.
Heedless of the wind and weather,
Fa la la la la, la la la la.

Copyright © 2002 by HAL LEONARD CORPORATION
International Copyright Secured   All Rights Reserved

Do They Know It's Christmas?

Words and Music by M. Ure and B. Geldof

It's Christmastime, there's no need to be afraid.
At Christmastime, we let in light and we banish shade.
And in our world of plenty we can spread a smile of joy.
Throw your arms around the world at Christmastime,
But say a prayer, to pray for the other ones at Christmastime.

It's hard, but when you're having fun,
There's a world outside your window.
And it's a world of dread and fear
Where the only water flowing is the bitter sting of tears.
And the Christmas bells that ring there
Are the clanging chimes of doom.
Well, tonight, thank God it's them instead of you.
And there won't be snow in Africa this Christmastime,
The greatest gift they'll get this year is life.
Oh, where nothing ever grows, no rain or rivers flow,
Do they know it's Christmastime at all?

Here's to you, raise a glass for everyone;
Here's to them, underneath that burning sun.
Do they know it's Christmastime at all?

Feed the world.
Feed the world.
Feed the world.
Let them know it's Christmastime again
Let them know it's Christmastime again.

Copyright © 1984 by M. Ure and B. Geldof
All Rights Administered by Chappell & Co.
International Copyright Secured   All Rights Reserved

Do You Hear What I Hear

Words and Music by Noel Regney and Gloria Shayne

Said the night wind to the little lamb,
"Do you see what I see?
Way up in the sky, little lamb,
Do you see what I see?
A star, a star, dancing in the night,
With a tail as big as a kite,
With a tail as big as a kite."

Said the little lamb to the shepherd boy,
"Do you hear what I hear?
Ringing through the sky, shepherd boy,
Do you hear what I hear?
A song, a song, high above the tree,
With a voice as big as the sea,
With a voice as big as the sea."

Said the shepherd boy to the mighty king,
"Do you know what I know?
In your palace warm, mighty king,
Do you know what I know?
A Child, a Child shivers in the cold;
Let us bring Him silver and gold,
Let us bring Him silver and gold."

Copyright © 1962 by Regent Music Corporation (BMI)
Copyright Renewed by Jewel Music Publishing Co., Inc. (ASCAP)
International Copyright Secured   All Rights Reserved
Used by Permission

Said the king to the people everywhere,
"Listen to what I say!
Pray for peace, people everywhere,
Listen to what I say!
The Child, the Child, sleeping in the night,
He will bring us goodness and light,
He will bring us goodness and light."

Don't Save It All for Christmas Day

Words and Music by Celine Dion, Peter Zizzo and Ric Wake

Don't get so busy that you miss
Giving a little kiss to the one you love.
Don't even wait a little while
To give 'em just a little smile.
A little is enough.
See how many people are crying.
Some people are dying.
How many people are asking for love?

So don't save it all for Christmas day.
Find a way to give a little love every day.
Don't save it all for Christmas day.
Find a way, 'cause holidays have come and gone,
But love lives on if you give on. Love.

How could you wait another minute?
A hug is warmer when you're in it;
Oh, baby, that's a fact.
But saying I love you's always better;
Seasons, reasons, they don't matter
So don't hold back.
See how many people in this world, so needed in this world?
How many people are praying for love?

Copyright © 1998 Duffield Corp., Connotation Music and Annotation Music
All Rights on behalf of Duffield Corp. Administered by Sony/ATV Music Publishing, 8 Music Square West,
    Nashville, TN 37203
All Rights on behalf of Connotation Music and Annotation Music Administered by Kobalt Music Services
International Copyright Secured   All Rights Reserved

So don't save it all for Christmas day.
Find a way to give a little love every day.
Don't save it all for Christmas day.
Find a way, 'cause holidays have come and gone,
But love lives on if you give on. Give love.

So let all the children know their whole life long.
Let them know love.
Find a way to give a little love every day.
Don't save it all for Christmas day.
Find a way to give a little love to everyone, everywhere.
Find a way 'cause holidays have come and gone,
But love lives on if you'll give on.
We've gotta give love, give love.

Feels Like Christmas

Words and Music by Pam Wendell and Elmo Shropshire

Old St. Nick and Mrs. Claus
Decided just this year
There won't be any Christmas.
The feeling's just not here.

Some kids get more than they need,
Some are spoiled rotten.
And when it comes to Christmas time,
Too many are forgotten.

It will feel like Christmas
To people everywhere,
It will feel like Christmas
When we all learn to share.

Santa said to Mrs. Claus,
"Something's way off track.
I can't get into Christmas
Until the spirit's back.

If there was just a way we could
Get boys and girls to see
Christmas is what's in our heart
And not what's 'neath the tree."

It will feel like Christmas
To people everywhere,
It will feel like Christmas
When we all learn to share.

Copyright © 1998 Elmo Publishing
International Copyright Secured   All Rights Reserved

Then all the kids said,
"Santa Claus, we have too many toys.
We'd like to share our blessings
With other girls and boys."

Now it feels like Christmas
To people everywhere.
And it feels like Christmas
Because we learned to share.

It will feel like Christmas
To people everywhere,
It will feel like Christmas
When we all learn to share.

Spoken: And will it feel like Christmas
When we've new things to wear?
No, it will
Sung: feel like Christmas
When we all learn to share.

Spoken: And will it feel like Christmas
When Doctor Elmo's on the air?
Oh, yes, it will feel like Christmas,
Sung: But we still should learn to share.

Feliz Navidad

Music and Lyrics by José Feliciano

Refrain:
Feliz Navidad.
Feliz Navidad.
Feliz Navidad.
Prospero año y felicidad.

Repeat Refrain

I want to wish you a Merry Christmas,
With lots of presents to make you happy.
I want to wish you a Merry Christmas
From the bottom of my heart.

I want to wish you a Merry Christmas,
With mistletoe and lots of cheer,
With lots of laughter throughout the years,
From the bottom of my heart.

Refrain

Copyright © 1970 J & H Publishing Company (ASCAP)
Copyright Renewed
All Rights Administered by Stollman and Stollman o/b/o J & H Publishing Company
International Copyright Secured   All Rights Reserved

The Friendly Beasts

Traditional English Carol

Jesus our brother, kind and good,
Was humbly born in a stable rude,
And the friendly beasts around Him stood,
Jesus our brother, kind and good.

"I," said the donkey, shaggy and brown,
"I carried His mother up hill and down;
I carried her safely to Bethlehem town."
"I," said the donkey, shaggy and brown.

"I," said the cow all white and red,
"I gave Him my manger for His bed;
I gave Him my hay to pillow His head."
"I," said the cow all white and red.

"I," said the sheep with curly horn,
"I gave Him my wool for His blanket warm;
He wore my coat on Christmas morn."
"I," said the sheep with curly horn.

"I," said the dove from the rafters high,
"I cooed Him to sleep so He would not cry;
We cooed Him to sleep, my mate and I."
"I," said the dove from the rafters high.

Thus every beast by some good spell,
In the stable dark was glad to tell
Of the gift he gave Emmanuel,
The gift he gave Emmanuel.

Copyright © 2002 by HAL LEONARD CORPORATION
International Copyright Secured   All Rights Reserved

The First Noel

17th Century English Carol
Music from W. Sandys' *Christmas Carols*

The first Noel, the angel did say,
Was to certain poor shepherds in fields as they lay;
In fields where they lay keeping their sheep,
On a cold winter's night that was so deep.
Noel, Noel, Noel, Noel,
Born is the King of Israel.

They looked up and saw a star
Shining in the East, beyond them far;
And to the earth it gave great light,
And so it continued both day and night.
Noel, Noel, Noel, Noel,
Born is the King of Israel.

And by the light of that same star,
Three wise men came from country far;
To seek for a King was their intent,
And to follow the star wherever it went.
Noel, Noel, Noel, Noel,
Born is the King of Israel.

This star drew nigh to the northwest,
O'er Bethlehem it took its rest;
And there it did doth stop and stay,
Right over the place where Jesus lay.
Noel, Noel, Noel, Noel,
Born is the King of Israel.

Copyright © 2002 by HAL LEONARD CORPORATION
International Copyright Secured   All Rights Reserved

Then entered in those wise men three,
Full reverently upon their knee;
And offered there in His presence,
Their gold, and myrrh, and frankincense.
Noel, Noel, Noel, Noel,
Born is the King of Israel.

Then let us all with one accord
Sing praises to our heav'nly Lord,
That hath made heav'n and earth of naught,
And with His blood mankind hath brought.
Noel, Noel, Noel, Noel,
Born is the King of Israel.

From Heaven Above to Earth I Come

Words and Music by Martin Luther

"From heav'n above to earth I come,
To bear good news to every home;
Glad tidings of great joy I bring,
Whereof I now will gladly sing.

"To you this night is born a Child
Of Mary, chosen mother mild;
This little Child of lowly birth
Shall be the joy of all the earth.

"'Tis Christ, our God, who far on high
Hath heard your sad and bitter cry;
Himself will your salvation be,
Himself from sin will make you free.

"He will on you the gifts bestow
Prepared by God for all below,
That in His kingdom, bright and fair,
You may with us His glory share.

"These are the tokens ye shall mark:
The swaddling-clothes and manger dark;
There ye shall find the Infant laid
By whom the heavens and earth were made."

Now let us all with gladsome cheer
Go with the shepherds and draw near
To see the precious gift of God,
Who hath His own dear Son bestowed.

Copyright © 2002 by HAL LEONARD CORPORATION
International Copyright Secured   All Rights Reserved

Give heed, my heart, lift up thine eyes!
What is it in yon manger lies?
Who is this child, so young and fair?
The blessed Christ-child lieth there.

Welcome to earth, Thou noble Guest,
Through whom e'en wicked men are blest!
Thou coms't to share our misery;
What can we render, Lord, to Thee?

Ah, Lord, who hast created all,
How weak art Thou, how poor and small,
That Thou dost choose Thine infant bed
Where humble cattle lately fed!

Were earth a thousand times as fair,
Beset with gold and jewels rare,
It yet were far too poor to be
A narrow cradle, Lord, for Thee.

For velvets soft and silken stuff
Thou hast but hay and straw so rough,
Whereon Thou, King, so rich and great,
As 'twere Thy heaven, art throned in state.

And thus, dear Lord, it pleaseth Thee
To make this truth quite plain to me,
That all the world's wealth, honor, might,
Are naught and worthless in Thy sight.

Ah, dearest Jesus, Holy Child,
Make Thee a bed, soft, undefiled,
Within my heart, that it may be
A quiet chamber kept for Thee.

My heart for very joy doth leap,
My lips no more can silence keep;
I too must sing with joyful tongue
That sweetest ancient cradle-song:

Glory to God in highest heav'n,
Who unto us His Son hath giv'n!
While angels sing with pious mirth
A glad new year to all the earth.

Fum, Fum, Fum

Traditional Catalonian Carol

On this joyful Christmas day
Sing fum, fum, fum.
On this joyful Christmas Day
Sing fum, fum, fum.
For a blessed Babe was born
Upon this day at break of morn.
In a manger poor and lowly
Lay the Son of God most holy.
Fum, fum, fum.

Thanks to God for holidays,
Sing fum, fum, fum.
Thanks to God for holidays,
Sing fum, fum, fum.
Now we all our voices raise
And sing a song of grateful praise,
Celebrate in song and story
All the wonders of His glory,
Fum, fum, fum.

Copyright © 2002 by HAL LEONARD CORPORATION
International Copyright Secured   All Rights Reserved

Frosty the Snow Man

Words and Music by Steve Nelson and Jack Rollins

Frosty the snow man
Was a jolly, happy soul,
With a corncob pipe and a button nose
And two eyes made out of coal.

Frosty the snow man
Is a fairy tale, they say;
He was made of snow, but the children know
How he came to life one day.

There must have been some magic
In that old silk hat they found,
For when they placed it on his head,
He began to dance around.

Oh, Frosty the snow man
Was alive as he could be,
And the children say he could laugh and play
Just the same as you and me.

Frosty the snowman
Knew the sun was hot that day,
So he said, "Let's run and we'll have some fun
Now before I melt away."

Down to the village
With a broomstick in his hand,
Running here and there all around the square,
Sayin', "Catch me if you can."

Copyright © 1950 by Chappell & Co.
Copyright Renewed
International Copyright Secured All Rights Reserved

He led them down the streets of town
Right to the traffic cop.
And he only paused a moment when
He heard him holler "Stop!"

For Frosty the snowman
Had to hurry on his way,
But he waved good-bye, sayin',
"Don't you cry, I'll be back again someday."

Thumpety thump thump,
Thumpety thump thump,
Look at Frosty go.
Thumpety thump thump,
Thumpety thump thump,
Over the hills of snow.

Gesù Bambino
(The Infant Jesus)

Text by Frederick H. Martens
Music by Pietro Yon

When blossoms flowered 'mid the snows,
Upon a winter night,
Was born the Child, the Christmas Rose,
The King of Love and Light.
The angels sang, the shepherds sang,
The grateful earth rejoiced,
And at His blessed birth
The stars their exultation voiced.

Refrain:
O come let us adore Him,
O come let us adore Him,
O come let us adore Him,
Christ the Lord.

Again the heart with rapture glows
To greet the holy night
That gave the world its Christmas Rose,
Its King of Love and Light.
Let every voice acclaim His name,
The grateful chorus swell,
From paradise to earth He came
That we with Him might dwell.

Refrain

Ah! O come let us adore Him,
Ah! Adore Him, Christ the Lord.
O come, o come, o come let us adore Him,
Let us adore Him, Christ the Lord.

Copyright © 2002 by HAL LEONARD CORPORATION
International Copyright Secured   All Rights Reserved

Go, Tell It on the Mountain

African-American Spiritual
Verses by John W. Work, Jr.

Refrain:
Go, tell it on the mountain,
Over the hills and everywhere;
Go, tell it on the mountain
That Jesus Christ is born.

While shepherds kept their watching
O'er silent flocks by night,
Behold, throughout the heavens,
There shone a holy light.

Refrain

The shepherds feared and trembled
When, lo! above the earth
Rang out the angel chorus
That hailed our Savior's birth.

Refrain

Down in a lowly manger
The humble Christ was born,
And God sent us salvation
That blessed Christmas morn.

Refrain

Copyright © 2002 by HAL LEONARD CORPORATION
International Copyright Secured   All Rights Reserved

The Gift

Words and Music by Tom Douglas and Jim Brickman

Female:
Winter snow is falling down,
Children laughing all around,
Lights are turning on,
Like a fairy tale come true.
Sitting by the fire we made,
You're the answer when I prayed
I would find someone
And, baby, I found you.

All I want is to hold you forever.
All I need is you more every day.
You saved my heart from being broken apart.
You gave your love away,
And I'm thankful every day for the gift.

Male:
Watching as you softly sleep,
What I'd give if I could keep
Just this moment,
If only time stood still.
But the colors fade away,
And the years will make us gray,
But, baby, in my eyes, you'll still be beautiful.

Both:
All I want is to hold you forever.
All I need is you more every day.

Copyright © 1997 Sony/ATV Songs LLC, Multisongs and Brickman Arrangement
All Rights on behalf of Sony/ATV Songs LLC Administered by Multisongs
International Copyright Secured All Rights Reserved

Male:
You saved my heart from being broken apart.

Female:
You gave your love away.

Male:
And I'm thankful every day.

Both:
For the gift.

Both:
All I want is to hold you forever.
All I need is you more every day.

Male:
You saved my heart from being broken apart.

Female:
You gave your love away.

Male:
I can't find the words to say.

Female:
That I'm thankful every day.

Both:
For the gift.

Gloria

Words and Music by Michael W. Smith
Based on "Angels We Have Heard on High"

Angels we have heard on high,
Sweetly singing o'er the plains.
And the mountains in reply
Echo back their joyous strains.

Refrain, Sing Twice:
Gloria, oh, gloria,
In excelsis Deo.
Gloria, oh, gloria,
In excelsis Deo.

Come to Bethlehem and see
Him whose birth the angels sing.
Come adore on bended knee
Christ the Lord, the newborn King.

Refrain Twice

Copyright © 1989 Sony/ATV Tunes LLC
All Rights Administered by Sony/ATV Music Publishing, 8 Music Square West, Nashville, TN 37203
International Copyright Secured   All Rights Reserved

Angels we have heard on high,
(Gloria, oh, sing gloria.)
Sweetly singing o'er the plains.
(Gloria, oh, sing gloria.)
Jesus, Lord of heav'n and earth;
With us sing our Savior's birth.

Refrain Three Times

Gloria, oh, gloria,
In excelsis Deo.
Alleluia!

God Rest Ye Merry, Gentlemen

19th Century English Carol

God rest ye merry, gentlemen,
Let nothing you dismay,
For Jesus Christ our Savior
Was born on upon this day,
To save us all from Satan's power
When we were gone astray.

Refrain:
O tidings of comfort and joy,
Comfort and joy;
O tidings of comfort and joy.

In Bethlehem, in Jewry,
This blessed Babe was born,
And laid within a manger
Upon this blessed morn;
To which His mother Mary
Did nothing take in scorn.
Refrain

From God our Heav'nly Father,
A blessed Angel came;
And unto certain shepherds
Brought tidings of the same;
How that in Bethlehem was born
The Son of God by Name.

Refrain

Copyright © 2002 by HAL LEONARD CORPORATION
International Copyright Secured   All Rights Reserved

Good Christian Men, Rejoice

14th Century Latin Text
Translated by John Mason Neale
14th Century German Melody

Good Christian men, rejoice,
With heart and soul and voice;
Give ye heed to what we say:
News! News! Jesus Christ is born today!
Ox and ass before him bow,
And He is in the manger now;
Christ is born today!
Christ is born today!

Good Christian men, rejoice,
With heart and soul and voice;
Now ye hear of endless bliss;
Joy! Joy! Jesus Christ was born for this!
He has ope'd the heav'nly door,
And man is blessed evermore.
Christ was born for this!
Christ was born for this!

Good Christian men, rejoice,
With heart and soul and voice;
Now ye need not fear the grave;
Peace! Peace! Jesus Christ was born to save!
Calls you one and calls you all,
To gain His everlasting hall.
Christ was born to save!
Christ was born to save!

Copyright © 2002 by HAL LEONARD CORPORATION
International Copyright Secured   All Rights Reserved

Good King Wenceslas

Words by John M. Neale
Music from *Piae Cantiones*

Good King Wenceslas look'd out
On the feast of Stephen,
When the snow lay round about,
Deep and crisp and even;
Brightly shone the moon that night,
Though the frost was cruel,
When a poor man came in sight,
Gath'ring winter fuel.

"Hither, page, and stand by me,
If thou know'st it, telling,
Yonder peasant, who is he?
Where and what his dwelling?"
"Sire, he lives a good league hence,
Underneath the mountain;
Right against the forest fence,
By Saint Agnes' fountain."

"Bring me flesh and bring me wine,
Bring me pine logs hither;
Thou and I will see him dine,
When we bear them thither."
Page and monarch, forth they went,
Forth they went together;
Through the rude wind's wild lament
And the bitter weather.

Copyright © 2002 by HAL LEONARD CORPORATION
International Copyright Secured   All Rights Reserved

"Sire, the night is darker now,
And the wind blows stronger;
Fails my heart, I know not how,
I can go no longer."
"Mark my footsteps, my good page;
Tread thou in them boldly:
Thou shalt find the winter's rage
Freeze thy blood less coldly."

In his master's steps he trod,
Where the snow lay dinted;
Heat was in the very sod
Which the saint had printed.
Therefore, Christian men, be sure,
Wealth or rank possessing,
Ye who now will bless the poor,
Shall yourselves find blessing.

Grandma Got Over by a Reindeer

Words and Music by Randy Brooks

Refrain:
Grandma got run over by a reindeer
Walking home from our house Christmas Eve.
You can say there's no such thing as Santa,
But as for me and Grandpa, we believe.

She'd been drinkin' too much eggnog
And we begged her not to go,
But she forgot her medication,
And she staggered out the door into the snow.
When we found her Christmas morning
At the scene of the attack,
She had hoofprints on her forehead
And incriminating Claus marks on her back.

Refrain

Now we're all so proud of Grandpa,
He's been taking this so well.
See him in there watching football,
Drinking beer and playing cards with Cousin Mel.
It's not Christmas without Grandma.
All the family's dressed in black,
And we just can't help but wonder:
Should we open up her gifts or send them back?

Refrain

Copyright © 1984 by Kris Publishing (SESAC) and Elmo Publishing (SESAC)
Admin. by ICG
All Rights Reserved   Used by Permission

Now the goose is on the table,
And the pudding made of fig,
And the blue and silver candles
That would just have matched the hair in Grandma's wig.
I've warned all my friends and neighbors,
Better watch out for yourselves.
They should never give a license
To a man who drives a sleigh and plays with elves.

Refrain

Grandma's Killer Fruitcake

Words and Music by Elmo Shropshire and Rita Abrams

The holidays were upon us
And things were goin' fine,
'Til the day I heard the doorbell
And a chill ran up my spine.
I grabbed the wife and children
As the postman wheeled it in;
A yearly Christmas nightmare
Had just come back again.

Refrain:
It was harder than the head of Uncle Bucky;
Heavy as a sermon of Preacher Lucky;
One's enough to give the whole state of Kentucky
A great big belly ache!
It was denser than a drove of barnyard turkeys;
Tougher than a truckload of all-beef jerky;
Drier than a drought in Albuquerque;
Grandma's killer fruitcake!

Now I had to swallow some marginal fare
At our family feast.
I even downed Aunt Dolly's possum pie
Just to keep the family peace.
I winced at Wilma's gizzard mousse,
But said it tasted fine.
But that lethal weapon Grandma baked
Is where I draw the line.

Copyright © 1992 Elmo Publishing and Mill Valley Music
International Copyright Secured   All Rights Reserved

Refrain

It's early Christmas mornin';
The phone rings us awake.
It's Grandma, Pa, she wants to know
How we liked the cake.
Well, Grandma, I never…we couldn't…
It was unbelievable, that's for sure!
What's that you say?
Oh, no Grandma, please!
Don't send us anymore!

Refrain Twice

Man, that's killer fruit…
Grandma's killer fruitcake.
Grandma's killer fruitcake!

The Greatest Gift of All

Words and Music by John Jarvis

Dawn is slowly breaking,
Our friends have all gone home.
You and I are waiting
For Santa Claus to come.
There's a present by the tree,
Stockings on the wall.
Knowing you're in love with me
Is the greatest gift of all.

The fire is slowly fading,
Chill is in the air.
All the gifts are waiting
For children everywhere.
Through the window I can see
Snow began to fall.
Knowing you're in love with me
Is the greatest gift of all.

Just before I go to sleep
I hear a church bell ring.
Merry Christmas everyone
Is the song it sings.
So I say a silent prayer
For creatures great and small.
Peace on earth, goodwill to men,
Is the greatest gift of all.
Peace on earth, goodwill to men,
Is the greatest gift of all.

Copyright © 1984 Sony/ATV Songs LLC
All Rights Administered by Sony/ATV Music Publishing, 8 Music Square West, Nashville, TN 37203
International Copyright Secured   All Rights Reserved

Greenwillow Christmas

By Frank Loesser

from *Greenwillow*

Three wise men followed a star one night
To where glad bells were pealing,
And soon beheld the Holy Child
And all the shepherds kneeling.

Refrain:
Come see the star, come hear the bells.
Come learn the tale this night forever tells.
Come one and all from far and wide.
Come know the joy, the joy, the joy.
Come know the joy of Christmastide.

'Twas long ago in Bethlehem
Yet ever live the glory,
And hearts all glow and voices rise
A-caroling the story.

Refrain

© 1959, 1960 (Renewed) FRANK MUSIC CORP.
All Rights Reserved

Happy Christmas, Little Friend

Lyrics by Oscar Hammerstein II
Music by Richard Rodgers

The soft morning light of a pale winter sun
Is tracing the trees on the snow.
Leap up, little friend, and fly down the stairs
For Christmas is waiting below.
There's a tree in the room running over with stars
That twinkle and sing to your eyes.
And under the tree there are presents that say,
Unwrap me and get a surprise.

Refrain:
Happy Christmas, little friend,
May your heart be laughing all day.
May your joy be a dream you'll remember,
As the years roll along on their way.
As the years roll along on their way,
You'll be showing your own kid a tree.
Then at last, my friend, you'll know
How happy a Christmas can be,
How happy a Christmas can be.

Repeat Refrain

Copyright © 1952 by The Rodgers & Hammerstein Foundation
Copyright Renewed
WILLIAMSON MUSIC owner of publication and allied rights throughout the world
International Copyright Secured   All Rights Reserved

Happy Holiday

Words and Music by Irving Berlin

from the Motion Picture *Irving Berlin's Holiday Inn*

Happy holiday, happy holiday.
While the merry bells keep ringing,
May your every wish come true.
Happy holiday, happy holiday.
May the calendar keep bringing
Happy holidays to you.

Repeat

© Copyright 1941, 1942 by Irving Berlin
Copyright Renewed
International Copyright Secured   All Rights Reserved

Happy Hanukkah, My Friend (The Hanukkah Song)

Words and Music by Justin Wilde and Douglas Alan Konecky

Spin the dreidel, light the lights,
Everyone stay home tonight.
The story is told,
The young and the old together.

As twilight greets the setting sun,
Light the candles one by one.
Remember the past,
Traditions that last forever.

Come, let's share the joy of Hanukkah.
May our friendship grow, as the candles glow.
Oh, won't you come and share the joy of Hanukkah;
And we'll celebrate as only friends can do.
Happy Hanukkah, my friend, from me to you.

Candlelight or star above,
Messages of peace and love;
Their meaning is clear,
We were put here as brothers.

So let's begin with you and me,
Let friendship shine eternally.
May this holiday
Enlighten the way for others.

Copyright © 1986 Songcastle Music and Cat's Whiskers Music/both admin. by ICG
International Copyright Secured All Rights Reserved

Come, let's share the joy of Hanukkah.
May our friendship grow, as the candles glow.
Oh, won't you come and share the joy of Hanukkah;
And we're hoping all you're wishing for comes true.
Happy Hanukkah, my friend, from me to you.
Happy Hanukkah, my friend, from me to you.

Happy New Year Darling

Music and Lyrics by Carmen Lombardo and Johnny Marks

Every time I hear "Auld Lang Syne,"
What memories it brings!
Crowds that flow, paper horns that blow,
And everybody sings:

Refrain:
Happy New Year, darling!
I give this toast to you.
Happy New Year, darling!
May all your dreams come true.
Let's always make believe
Each night is New Year's Eve.
Then we'll always find
Our troubles far behind.
New year's resolutions
Were made to break, they say,
But I'll keep my promise
To love you more each day.
Let's ring out the old year
And ring in the new
With happy New Year, darling, to you!

Refrain

Copyright © 1946 (Renewed 1973) St. Nicholas Music Inc., 1619 Broadway, New York, New York 10019
All Rights Reserved

He

Words by Richard Mullen
Music by Jack Richards

He can turn the tides and calm the angry sea;
He alone decides who writes a symphony;
He lights every star that makes our darkness bright,
He keeps watch all through each long and lonely night.

He still finds the time to hear a child's first prayer;
Saint or sinner call and always find him there.
Though it makes him sad to see the way we live,
He'll always say, "I forgive."

He can grant a wish or make a dream come true,
He can paint the clouds and turn the gray to blue;
He alone knows where to find the rainbow's end,
He alone can see what lies beyond the bend.

He can touch a tree and turn the leaves to gold,
He knows every lie that you and I have told.
Though it makes him sad to see the way we live,
He'll always say, "I forgive, I forgive."

© 1954, 1969 AVAS MUSIC PUBLISHING CO., INC.
© Renewed 1982 WAROCK CORP. and AVAS MUSIC PUBLISHING CO., INC.
All Rights Reserved

Happy Xmas (War Is Over)

Words and Music by John Lennon and Yoko Ono

So this is Xmas
And what have you done?
Another year over,
And a new one just begun;
And so this is Xmas,
I hope you have fun,
The near and the dear ones,
The old and the young.

Refrain:
A merry, merry Xmas
And a happy New Year.
Let's hope it's a good one
Without any fear.

And so this is Xmas
For weak and for strong,
The rich and the poor ones,
The road is so long.
And so, happy Xmas
For black and for white,
For the yellow and red ones,
Let's stop all the fights.

Refrain

© 1971 (Renewed 1999) LENONO.MUSIC and ONO MUSIC
All Rights Controlled and Administered by EMI BLACKWOOD MUSIC INC.
All Rights Reserved   International Copyright Secured   Used by Permission

So this is Xmas
And what have we done?
Another year over,
And a new one just begun;
And so this is Xmas,
We hope you have fun,
The near and the dear ones,
The old and the young.

Refrain

War is over if you want it,
War is over now.

Hard Candy Christmas

Words and Music by Carol Hall

from *The Best Little Whorehouse In Texas*

Hey, maybe I'll dye my hair,
Maybe I'll move somewhere.
Maybe I'll get a car,
Maybe I'll drive so far they'll all lose track.
Me, I'll bounce right back.

Maybe I'll sleep real late,
Maybe I'll lose some weight.
Maybe I'll clear the junk,
Maybe I'll just get drunk on apple wine.
Me, I'll be just fine and dandy.

Lord, it's like a hard candy Christmas.
I'm barely getting through tomorrow,
Still I won't let sorrow bring me down.
I'll be fine and dandy.
Lord, it's like a hard candy Christmas.
I'm barely getting through tomorrow,
Still I won't let sorrow bring me way down.

Hey, maybe I'll learn to sew,
Maybe I'll just lie low.
Maybe I'll hit the bars,
Maybe I'll count the stars until the dawn.
Me, I will go on.

Copyright © 1977, 1978 DANIEL MUSIC LTD. and OTAY MUSIC CORP.
Copyright Renewed
All Rights for the United States and Canada Controlled and Administered by UNIVERSAL MUSIC CORP.
All Rights Reserved   Used by Permission

Maybe I'll settle down,
Maybe I'll just leave town.
Maybe I'll have some fun,
Maybe I'll meet someone and make 'em mine.
Me, I'll just be fine and dandy.

Lord, it's like a hard candy Christmas.
I'm barely getting through tomorrow,
Still I won't let sorrow bring me down.
I'll be fine and dandy.
Lord, it's like a hard candy Christmas.
I'm barely getting through tomorrow,
Still I won't let sorrow bring me way down.
I'll be fine. I'll be fine.

Hark! The Herald Angels Sing

Words by Charles Wesley
Altered by George Whitefield
Music by Felix Mendelssohn-Bartholdy

Hark! the herald angels sing,
"Glory to the newborn King!
Peace on earth, and mercy mild,
God and sinners reconciled!"
Joyful, all ye nations, rise,
Join the triumph of the skies;
With th'angelic host proclaim,
"Christ is born in Bethlehem!"
Hark! the herald angels sing,
"Glory to the newborn King!"

Christ, by highest heav'n adored,
Christ the everlasting Lord;
Late in time behold Him come,
Offspring of the virgin womb.
Veiled in flesh, the Godhead see:
Hail, th'incarnate Deity;
Pleased, as man, with men to dwell,
Jesus, our Emmanuel!
Hark! the herald angels sing,
"Glory to the newborn King!"

Copyright © 2002 by HAL LEONARD CORPORATION
International Copyright Secured   All Rights Reserved

Hail, the heav'n-born Prince of peace!
Hail, the Son of Righteousness!
Light and life to all He brings,
Ris'n with healing in his wings.
Mild He lays His glory by,
Born that man no more may die,
Born to raise the sons of earth,
Born to give them second birth.
Hark! the herald angels sing,
"Glory to the newborn King!"

He Is Born, the Holy Child (Il est ne, le divin Enfant)

Traditional French Carol

Refrain:
He is born, the holy Child,
Play the oboe and bagpipes merrily!
He is born, the holy Child,
Sing we all of the Savior mild.

Through long ages of the past,
Prophets have betold His coming;
Through long ages of the past,
Now the time has come at last!

Refrain

O how lovely, o how pure
Is this perfect Child of heaven;
O how lovely, O how pure,
Gracious gift of God to man!

Refrain

Jesus, Lord of all the world,
Coming as a Child among us;
Jesus, Lord of all the world,
Grant to us Thy heav'nly peace.

Refrain

Copyright © 2002 by HAL LEONARD CORPORATION
International Copyright Secured   All Rights Reserved

Here We Come A-Wassailing

Traditional

Here we come a-wassailing
Among the leaves so green,
Here we come a-wand'ring,
So fair to be seen.

Refrain:
Love and joy come to you,
And to your wassail too;
And God bless you and send you
A happy New Year,
And God send you
A happy New Year.

We are not daily beggars
That beg from door to door,
But we are neighbors' children,
Whom you have seen before.
Refrain

We have got a little purse
Of stretching leather skin;
We want a little money
To line it well within.
Refrain

God bless the master of this house,
Likewise the mistress too,
And all the little children
That round the table go.
Refrain

Copyright © 2002 by HAL LEONARD CORPORATION
International Copyright Secured   All Rights Reserved

Here Comes Santa Claus
(Right Down Santa Claus Lane)

Words and Music by Gene Autry and Oakley Haldeman

Here comes Santa Claus! Here comes Santa Claus!
Right down Santa Claus Lane!
Vixen and Blitzen and all his reindeer
Are pulling on the rein.

Bells are ringing, children singing,
All is merry and bright.
Hang your stockings and say your prayers,
'Cause Santa Claus comes tonight.

Here comes Santa Claus! Here comes Santa Claus!
Right down Santa Claus Lane!
He's got a bag that is filled with toys
For the boys and girls again.

Hear those sleighbells jingle jangle,
What a beautiful sight.
Jump in bed, cover up your head,
'Cause Santa Claus comes tonight.

Here comes Santa Claus! Here comes Santa Claus!
Right down Santa Claus Lane!
He doesn't care if you're rich or poor,
For he loves you just the same.

© 1947 (Renewed) Gene Autry's Western Music Publishing Co.
All Rights Reserved   Used by Permission

Santa knows that we're God's children;
That makes everything right.
Fill your hearts with a Christmas cheer,
'Cause Santa Claus comes tonight.

Here comes Santa Claus! Here comes Santa Claus!
Right down Santa Claus Lane!
He'll come around when the chimes ring out;
Then it's Christmas morn again.

Peace on earth will come to all
If we just follow the light.
Let's give thanks to the Lord above,
'Cause Santa Claus comes tonight.

The Holly and the Ivy

18th Century English Carol

The holly and the ivy,
When they are both full grown,
Of all the trees that are in the wood,
The holly bears the crown.

Refrain:
The rising of the sun
And the running of the deer,
The playing of the merry organ,
Sweet singing in the choir.

The holly bears a blossom
As white as lily flow'r,
And Mary bore sweet Jesus Christ
To be our dear Savior.

Refrain

The holly bears a berry
As red as any blood,
And Mary bore sweet Jesus Christ
To do poor sinners good.

Refrain

Copyright © 2002 by HAL LEONARD CORPORATION
International Copyright Secured   All Rights Reserved

The holly bears a prickle
As sharp as any thorn,
And Mary bore sweet Jesus Christ
On Christmas day in the morn.

Refrain

The holly bears a bark
As bitter as the gall,
And Mary bore sweet Jesus Christ
For to redeem us all.

Refrain

Repeat Verse 1 and Refrain

A Holly Jolly Christmas

Music and Lyrics by Johnny Marks

Have a holly jolly Christmas,
It's the best time of the year.
I don't know if there'll be snow
But have a cup of cheer.

Have a holly jolly Christmas,
And when you walk down the street,
Say hello to friends you know
And everyone you meet.

Oh, ho, the mistletoe
Hung where you can see,
Somebody waits for you,
Kiss her once for me.

Have a holly jolly Christmas,
And in case you didn't hear,
Oh, by golly, have a holly jolly
Christmas this year.

Repeat All

Copyright © 1962, 1964 (Renewed 1990, 1992) St. Nicholas Music Inc., 1619 Broadway, New York,
    New York 10019
All Rights Reserved

I Heard the Bells on Christmas Day

Words by Henry Wadsworth Longfellow
Adapted by Johnny Marks
Music by Johnny Marks

I heard the bells on Christmas day,
Their old familiar carols play,
And mild and sweet the words repeat,
Of peace on earth, goodwill to men.

I thought how as the day had come,
The belfries of all Christendom
Had rung so long the unbroken song
Of peace on earth, goodwill to men.

And in despair I bowed my head:
"There is no peace on earth," I said,
"For hate is strong, and mocks the song
Of peace on earth, goodwill to men."

Then pealed the bells more loud and deep:
"God is not dead, nor doth He sleep;
The wrong shall fail, the right prevail,
With peace on earth, goodwill to men."

Copyright © 1956 (Renewed 1984) St. Nicholas Music Inc., 1619 Broadway, New York, New York 10019
All Rights Reserved

(There's No Place Like) Home for the Holidays

Words by Al Stillman Music by Robert Allen

Refrain 1:
Oh, there's no place like home for the holidays,
'Cause no matter how far away you roam,
When you pine for the sunshine of a friendly gaze,
For the holidays you can't beat home, sweet home.

I met a man who lives in Tennessee,
And he was headin' for
Pennsylvania and some homemade pumpkin pie.
From Pennsylvania folks are trav'lin'
Down to Dixie's sunny shore;
From Atlantic to Pacific, gee,
The traffic is terrific!

Refrain 2:
Oh, there's no place like home for the holidays,
'Cause no matter how far away you roam,
If you want to be happy in a million ways,
For the holidays you can't beat home, sweet home.

Refrain 1

© Copyright 1954 Roncom Music Co.
Copyright Renewed 1982 and Assigned to Charlie Deitcher Productions, Inc. and Kitty Anne Music Co.
International Copyright Secured   All Rights Reserved

A home that knows your joy and laughter filled
With mem'ries by the score
Is a home you're glad to welcome with your heart.
From California to New England
Down to Dixie's sunny shore;
From Atlantic to Pacific, gee,
The traffic is terrific!

Refrain 2

I Saw Mommy Kissing Santa Claus

Words and Music by Tommie Connor

I saw Mommy kissing Santa Claus
Underneath the mistletoe last night.
She didn't see me creep
Down the stairs to have a peep,
She thought that I was tucked up in my bedroom fast asleep.
Then I saw Mommy tickle Santa Claus,
Underneath his beard so snowy white.
Oh, what a laugh it would have been
If Daddy had only seen
Mommy kissing Santa Claus last night.

Copyright © 1952 by Regent Music Corporation (BMI)
Copyright Renewed by Jewel Music Publishing Co., Inc. (ASCAP)
International Copyright Secured   All Rights Reserved
Used by Permission

I Wish Everyday Could Be Like Christmas

Words and Music by David Erwin and Jim Carter

Once a year there comes a time when love is in the air.
Everywhere you look, you see a smile.
Friendly faces say that someone really cares.
I wish it could last forever, and not just for awhile.

Fires burning warmer even though snow is on the ground.
Stars are shining brighter in the sky.
That very special day is about to come around,
When God smiles down from heaven and the whole world comes alive.

I wish every day could be like Christmas,
And every night like Christmas Eve.
I wish every day could be like Christmas,
And I know it could if we would just believe.

Children sing and play while they wait for their surprise.
Their laughter sounds just like a happy song.
If only we could see the world through children's eyes,
We would have the spirit of Christmas all the whole year long.

I wish every day could be like Christmas,
And every night like Christmas Eve.
I wish every day could be like Christmas,
And I know it could if we would just believe.

I wish every day could be like Christmas,
And I know it could if we would just believe.

Copyright © 1983 UNIVERSAL - POLYGRAM INTERNATIONAL PUBLISHING, INC.
All Rights Reserved   Used by Permission

I Saw Three Ships

Traditional English Carol

I saw three ships come sailing in
On Christmas day, on Christmas day;
I saw three ships come sailing in
On Christmas day in the morning.

And what was in those ships all three
On Christmas day, on Christmas day?
And what was in those ships all three
On Christmas day in the morning?

Our Savior Christ and His lady
On Christmas day, on Christmas day.
Our Savior Christ and His lady
On Christmas day in the morning.

Pray, whither sailed those ships all three
On Christmas day, on Christmas day?
Pray, whither sailed those ships all three
On Christmas day, on Christmas day?

O, they sailed into Bethlehem
On Christmas day, on Christmas day;
O, they sailed into Bethlehem
On Christmas day in the morning.

Copyright © 2002 by HAL LEONARD CORPORATION
International Copyright Secured   All Rights Reserved

And all the bells on earth shall ring
On Christmas day, on Christmas day;
And all the bells on earth shall ring
On Christmas day in the morning.

And all the angels in heav'n shall sing
On Christmas day, on Christmas day;
And all the angels in heav'n shall sing
On Christmas day in the morning.

And all the souls on earth shall sing
On Christmas day, on Christmas day;
And all the souls on earth shall sing
On Christmas day in the morning.

Then let us all rejoice amain
On Christmas day, on Christmas day;
Then let us all rejoice amain
On Christmas day in the morning!

I Wonder as I Wander

By John Jacob Niles

I wonder as I wander out under the sky,
How Jesus the Savior did come for to die.
For poor on'ry people like you and like I.
I wonder as I wander out under the sky.

When Mary birthed Jesus, 'twas in a cow's stall,
With wise men and farmers and shepherds and all.
But high from God's heaven a star's light did fall,
And the promise of ages it then did recall.

If Jesus had wanted for any wee thing,
A star in the sky or a bird on the wing,
Or all of God's angels in heav'n for to sing,
He surely could have it, 'cause He was the King.

Repeat Verse 1

Copyright © 1934 (Renewed) by G. Schirmer, Inc. (ASCAP), New York, NY
International Copyright Secured   All Rights Reserved
Reprinted by Permission

I'll Be Home for Christmas

Words and Music by Kim Gannon and Walter Kent

I'm dreaming tonight of a place I love,
Even more than I usually do.
And although I know it's a long road back,
I promise you.

I'll be home for Christmas,
You can count on me.
Please have snow and mistletoe
And presents on the tree.
Christmas Eve will find me
Where the lovelight gleams,
I'll be home for Christmas
If only in my dreams.

© Copyright 1943 by Gannon & Kent Music Co., Inc., Beverly Hills, CA
Copyright Renewed
International Copyright Secured   All Rights Reserved

I've Got My Love to Keep Me Warm

Words and Music by Irving Berlin

from the 20th Century Fox Motion Picture *On the Avenue*

The snow is snowing,
The wind is blowing,
But I can weather the storm.
What do I care how much it may storm?
I've got my love to keep me warm.

I can't remember
A worse December;
Just watch those icicles form.
What do I care if icicles form?
I've got my love to keep me warm.

Off with my overcoat,
Off with my glove.
I need no overcoat,
I'm burning with love.

My heart's on fire,
The flame grows higher.
So I will weather the storm.
What do I care how much it may storm?
I've got my love to keep me warm.

© Copyright 1936, 1937 by Irving Berlin
© Arrangement Copyright 1948 by Irving Berlin
Copyright Renewed
International Copyright Secured   All Rights Reserved

Infant Holy, Infant Lowly

Traditional Polish Carol
Paraphrased by Edith M.G. Reed

Infant holy, Infant lowly,
For His bed a cattle stall.
Oxen lowing, little knowing
Christ the Babe is Lord of all.
Swift are winging angels singing,
Noels ringing, tidings bringing:
Christ the Babe is Lord of all.

Flocks are sleeping, shepherds keeping
Vigil till the morning new,
Saw the glory, heard the story,
Tidings of a Gospel true.
Thus rejoicing, free from sorrow,
Praises voicing greet the morrow:
Christ the Babe was born for you.

Copyright © 2002 by HAL LEONARD CORPORATION
International Copyright Secured   All Rights Reserved

It Came Upon the Midnight Clear

Words by Edmund H. Sears
Traditional English Melody

It came upon the midnight clear,
That glorious song of old,
From angels bending near the earth
To touch their harps of gold:
"Peace on the earth, goodwill to men,
From heav'n's all-gracious King."
The world in solemn stillness lay
To hear the angels sing.

Still through the cloven skies they came
With peaceful wings unfurled,
And still their heavenly music floats
O'er all the weary world;
Above its sad and lowly plains,
They bend on hovering wing.
And ever o'er its Babel sounds
The blessed angels sing.

And ye, beneath life's crushing load,
Whose forms are bending low,
Who toil along the climbing way
With painful steps and slow,
Look now! For glad and golden hours
Come swiftly on the wing.
O rest beside the weary road,
And hear the angels sing.

Copyright © 2002 by HAL LEONARD CORPORATION
International Copyright Secured   All Rights Reserved

For lo! The days are hastening on,
By prophet seen of old,
When, with the ever-circling years,
Shall come the time foretold
When peace shall over all the earth
Its ancient splendors fling,
And the whole world send back the song
Which now the angels sing.

It Must Have Been the Mistletoe (Our First Christmas)

By Justin Wilde and Doug Konecky

It must have been the mistletoe,
The lazy fire, the falling snow,
The magic in the frosty air,
That feeling everywhere.
It must have been the pretty lights
That glistened in the silent night,
Or maybe just the stars so bright
That shined above you.

Our first Christmas,
More than we'd been dreaming of.
Old Saint Nich'las had his fingers crossed
That we would fall in love.

It could have been the holiday,
The midnight ride upon a sleigh,
The countryside all dressed in white,
That crazy snowball fight.
It could have been the steeple bell
That wrapped us up within its spell.
It only took one kiss to know,
It must have been the mistletoe.

Our first Christmas,
More than we'd been dreaming of.
Old Saint Nich'las must have known that kiss
Would lead to all of this.

© Copyright 1979 Songcastle Music (ASCAP) and Cat's Whiskers Music (ASCAP)/both admin. by ICG
All Rights Reserved   Used by Permission

It must have been the mistletoe,
The lazy fire, the falling snow,
The magic in the frosty air,
That made me love you.
On Christmas Eve a wish came true,
That night I fell in love with you.
It only took one kiss to know,
It must have been the mistletoe.
It must have been the mistletoe.
It must have been the mistletoe.

It's Beginning to Look Like Christmas

By Meredith Willson

It's beginning to look a lot like Christmas,
Everywhere you go.
Take a look in the five and ten,
Glistening once again,
With candy canes and silver lanes aglow.

It's beginning to look a lot like Christmas,
Toys in every store.
But the prettiest sight to see
Is the holly that will be
On your own front door.

A pair of hopalong boots
And a pistol that shoots
Is the wish of Barney and Ben;
Dolls that will talk
And will go for a walk
Is the hope of Janice and Jen;
And Mom and Dad can hardly wait
For school to start again.

© 1951 PLYMOUTH MUSIC CO., INC.
© Renewed 1979 FRANK MUSIC CORP. and MEREDITH WILLSON MUSIC
All Rights Reserved

It's beginning to look a lot like Christmas,
Everywhere you go.
There's a tree in the Grand Hotel,
One in the park as well,
The sturdy kind that doesn't mind the snow.

It's beginning to look a lot like Christmas,
Soon the bells will start.
And the thing that will make them ring
Is the carol that you sing
Right within your heart.

It's Christmas in New York

Words and Music by Billy Butt

Church bells are ringing,
Choirs are singing,
Joy they are bringing,
It's Christmas in New York.
Streetlights are pleasing,
Snowflakes are teasing,
Central Park's freezing,
It's Christmas in New York.
The stars in the heavens are so bright
They tell of a baby that was born in night.

Rest'rant signs swaying,
Blue skies are graying,
Everyone's saying,
It's Christmas in New York.
Skyscrapers gleaming,
Broadway lights beaming,
Children are dreaming,
It's Christmas in New York.
The lights on the Christmas tree are fine,
The sights of the shopping sprees, the gifts, yours and mine.

Copyright © 1986 by Billybee Songs and Misty Music AB, Stockholm, Sweden
Administered in the United States and Canada by Galahad Music, Inc.
International Copyright Secured   All Rights Reserved

Stockings are filling,
Champagne is chilling,
It's all so thrilling,
It's Christmas in New York.
Log fires are burning,
Santa's returning
Feeling each yearning,
It's Christmas in New York.

Church bells are ringing,
Choirs are singing,
Joy they are bringing,
It's Christmas in New York,
It's Christmas in New York,
It's Christmas in New York.

It's Christmas Time
All Over the World

Words and Music by Hugh Martin

It's Christmas time all over the world,
And Christmas here at home.
The church bells chime wherever we roam,
So "Joyeux Noël," "Feliz Natal," "Gellukkig Kerstfeest" to you!

The snow is thick in most of the world
And children's eyes are wide
As old Saint Nick gets ready to ride,
So "Feliz Navidad," "Cracium Fericit," and "Happy New Year" to you!

Though the customs may change,
And the language is strange,
This appeal we feel is real
In Holland or Hong Kong.

It's Christmas time all over the world,
In places near and far;
And so, my friends, wherever you are,
A "Fröhliche Weihnachten!" "Kala Christougena!" "Yoi Kurisumasu!"
Which means a very merry Christmas to you!

TRO - © Copyright 1965 (Renewed) Cromwell Music, Inc., New York, NY
International Copyright Secured
All Rights Reserved Including Public Performance For Profit
Used by Permission

Jesus Is Born

Words and Music by Steve Green, Phil Naish and Colleen Green

Refrain (Sing Twice):
The bells are ringing, people are singing,
Angels say with joy, "Jesus is born!"
There in a manger, He was no stranger.
Prophesied, now alive, Jesus is born!

Behold the gift of salvation,
A light for all to see,
Revealing all God's glory,
Emmanuel is He.

Behold the gift of salvation
In Christ the Promised One.
Shining through the darkness,
Jesus Christ has come.

Refrain Twice

Glory to the King, Lord of everything,
Christ has finally come.
Glory to the King, let the people sing
Hallelujah, Hallelujah.

Refrain Twice

Glorified, still alive, Jesus is born!
Glorified, still alive, Jesus is born!

© 1987 BIRDWING MUSIC (ASCAP), PAMELA KAY MUSIC (ASCAP), BECKENGUS MUSIC (BMI) and
   BMG SONGS (ASCAP)
BIRDWING MUSIC, PAMELA KAY MUSIC and BECKENGUS MUSIC Admin. by EMI CMG PUBLISHING
All Rights Reserved   Used by Permission

It's Just Another New Year's Eve

Lyric by Marty Panzer
Music by Barry Manilow

Don't look so sad.
It's not so bad, you know.
It's just another night,
That's all it is.
It's not the first.
It's not the worst, you know.
We've come through all the rest.
We'll get through this.

We've made mistakes,
But we've made good friends, too.
Remember all the nights
We've spent with them.
And all our plans,
Who says they can't come true?
Tonight's another chance
To start again.

Copyright © 1977 by Careers-BMG Music Publishing and SwaneeBRAVO! Music
Copyright Renewed
All Rights Administered by Careers-BMG Music Publishing
International Copyright Secured   All Rights Reserved

Refrain:
It's just another New Year's Eve,
Another night like all the rest.
It's just another New Year's Eve,
Let's make it the best.
It's just another New Year's Eve
It's just another Auld Lang Syne.
But when we're through
This New Year you'll see
We'll be just fine.

We're not alone,
We've got the world, you know.
And it won't let us down,
Just wait and see.
And we'll grow old,
But think how wise we'll grow.
There's more, you know,
It's only New Year's Eve.

Refrain

Jingle-Bell Rock

Words and Music by Joe Beal and Jim Boothe

Jingle-bell, jingle-bell, jingle-bell rock,
Jingle-bells swing and jingle-bells ring.
Snowin' and blowin' up bushels of fun,
Now the jingle hop has begun.

Jingle-bell, jingle-bell, jingle-bell rock,
Jingle bells chime in jingle-bell time.
Dancin' and prancin' in Jingle Bell Square
In the frosty air.

What a bright time, it's the right time,
To rock the night away.
Jingle-bell time is a swell time
To go glidin' in a one-horse sleigh.

Giddy-ap jingle horse, pick up your feet,
Jingle around the clock.
Mix and mingle in a jinglin' beat,
That's the jingle-bell rock.

Copyright © 1957 by Chappell & Co.
Copyright Renewed
International Copyright Secured   All Rights Reserved

Jolly Old St. Nicholas

Traditional 19th Century American Carol

Jolly old Saint Nicholas,
Lean your ear this way.
Don't you tell a single soul
What I'm going to say.
Christmas Eve is coming soon,
Now, you dear old man,
Whisper what you'll bring to me;
Tell me if you can.

When the clock is striking twelve,
When I'm fast asleep,
Down the chimney broad and black,
With your pack you'll creep.
All the stockings you will find
Hanging in a row.
Mine will be the shortest one,
You'll be sure to know.

Johnny wants a pair of skates;
Susy wants a sled;
Nellie wants a picture book,
Yellow, blue, and red;
Now I think I'll leave to you
What to give the rest.
Choose for me, dear Santa Claus,
You will know the best.

Copyright © 2002 by HAL LEONARD CORPORATION
International Copyright Secured   All Rights Reserved

Jingle Bells

Words and Music by J. Pierpont

Dashing through the snow,
In a one-horse open sleigh,
O'er the fields we go,
Laughing all the way.
Bells on bobtail ring,
Making spirits bright,
What fun it is to ride and sing
A sleighing song tonight! Oh!

Refrain:
Jingle bells, jingle bells,
Jingle all the way.
Oh what fun it is to ride
In a one-horse open sleigh!
Jingle bells, jingle bells,
Jingle all the way.
Oh what fun it is to ride
In a one-horse open sleigh!

A day or two ago
I thought I'd take a ride,
And soon Miss Fanny Bright
Was seated by my side.
The horse was lean and lank,
Misfortune seemed his lot,
He got into a drifted bank
And we, we got upset! Oh!

Copyright © 2002 by HAL LEONARD CORPORATION
International Copyright Secured   All Rights Reserved

Refrain

Now the ground is white,
Go it while you're young.
And take the girls tonight
And sing this sleighing song.
Just get a bobtail bay,
Two-forty for his speed,
Then hitch him to an open sleigh
And crack, you'll take the lead! Oh!

Refrain

Joy to the World

Words by Isaac Watts
Music by George Frideric Handel
Arranged by Lowell Mason

Joy to the world! The Lord is come;
Let earth receive her King;
Let every heart prepare Him room,
And heav'n and nature sing,
And heav'n and nature sing,
And heav'n and heav'n and nature sing.

Joy to the earth! The Savior reigns;
Let men their songs employ;
While fields and floods, rocks, hills and plains
Repeat the sounding joy,
Repeat the sounding joy,
Repeat, repeat the sounding joy.

No more let sin and sorrows grow,
Nor thorns infest the ground;
He comes to make His blessings flow
Far as the curse is found,
Far as the curse is found,
Far as, far as the curse is found.

He rules the world with truth and grace,
And makes the nations prove
The glories of His righteousness
And wonders of His love,
And wonders of His love,
And wonders, wonders of His love.

Copyright © 2002 by HAL LEONARD CORPORATION
International Copyright Secured   All Rights Reserved

Let It Snow! Let It Snow! Let It Snow!

Words by Sammy Cahn
Music by Jule Styne

Oh, the weather outside is frightful,
But the fire is so delightful,
And since we've no place to go,
Let it snow! Let it snow! Let it snow!

It doesn't show signs of stopping,
And I brought some corn for popping,
The lights are turned way down low,
Let it snow! Let it snow! Let it snow!

When we finally kiss goodnight,
How I'll hate going out in the storm!
But if you'll really hold me tight,
All the way home I'll be warm.

The fire is slowly dying
And, my dear, we're still good-bye-ing,
But as long as you love me so,
Let it snow! Let it snow! Let it snow!

Copyright © 1945 by Producers Music Publishing Co. and Cahn Music Company
Copyright Renewed
All Rights for Producers Music Publishing Co. Administered by Chappell & Co.
International Copyright Secured   All Rights Reserved

Last Christmas

Words and Music by George Michael

Spoken: Happy Christmas.
Sung: Ah, ooh, whoa, ah.

Refrain (Sing twice):
Last Christmas I gave you my heart,
But the very next day you gave it away.
This year, to save me from tears,
I'll give it to someone special.

Once bitten and twice shy,
I keep my distance but tears still catch my eye.
Tell me, baby, do you recognize me?
Well, it's been a year. It doesn't surprise me.
Happy Christmas. I wrapped it up and sent it
With a note saying, "I love you." I meant it.
Now I know what a fool I've been.
But if you kissed me now I know you'd fool me again.

Refrain Twice

A crowded room, friends with tired eyes.
I'm hiding from you and your soul of ice.
My god, I thought you were someone to rely on.
Me, I guess I was a shoulder to cry on.
A face on a lover with a fire in his heart,
A man under cover but you tore me apart.
Ooh, now I've found a real love.
You'll never fool me again.

Copyright © 1985 by Morrison-Leahy Music Ltd.
Published in the U.S.A. by Chappell & Co.
International Copyright Secured   All Rights Reserved

Refrain Twice

A face on a lover with a fire in his heart,
A man under cover but you tore him apart.
Maybe next year I'll give it to someone,
I'll give it to someone special, special.

Repeat and Fade:
Someone, someone. I'll give it to someone,
I'll give it someone special.

The Last Month of the Year (What Month Was Jesus Born In?)

Words and Music by Vera Hall
Adapted and Arranged by Ruby Pickens Tartt and Alan Lomax

What month was my Jesus born in?
Last month of the year!
What month was my Jesus born in?
Last month of the year!

Refrain:
Oh, January, February, March,
April, May, June, oh Lord,
You got July, August, September,
October, and a November,
On the twenty-fifth day of December
In the last month of the year.

Well, they laid him in a manger,
Last month of the year!
Well, they laid him in a manger,
Last month of the year!

Refrain

TRO - © Copyright 1960 (Renewed) Ludlow Music, Inc., New York, NY
International Copyright Secured
All Rights Reserved Including Public Performance For Profit
Used by Permission

Wrapped Him up in swaddling clothing,
Last month of the year!
Wrapped Him up in swaddling clothing,
Last month of the year!

Refrain

Well, He was born of the Virgin Mary,
Last month of the year!
He was born of the Virgin Mary,
Last month of the year!

Refrain

Let's Have an Old Fashioned Christmas

Lyric by Larry Conley
Music by Joe Solomon

Another year has rolled around,
In spite of everything;
So let's make use of one excuse
To love and laugh and sing:

Refrain:
Let's have an old-fashioned Christmas,
Dress up an old-fashioned tree;
Let's make the spirit of Auld Lang Syne
The same as it used to be;
Hearts will be light as a feather
After some old-fashioned cheer;
So let's all be good fellows together,
Let's have an old-fashioned Christmas this year.

Repeat Refrain

© 1939 (Renewed) EDWIN H. MORRIS & COMPANY, A Division of MPL Music Publishing, Inc.
All Rights Reserved

Little Altar Boy

Words and Music by Howlett Smith

Little altar boy, I wonder could you pray for me?
Little altar boy, for I have gone astray.
What must I do to be holy like you?
Little altar boy, oh, let me hear you pray.

Little altar boy, I wonder could you ask our Lord?
Ask Him, altar boy, to take my sins away.
What must I do to be holy like you?
Little altar boy, please let me hear you pray.

Lift up your voice and sing a prayer above.
Help me rejoice and fill that prayer with love.
Now I know my life has been all wrong.
Lift up your voice and help a sinner be strong.

Little altar boy, I wonder could you pray for me?
Could you tell our Lord I'm gonna change my way today?
What must I do to be holy like you?
Little altar boy, oh, let me hear you pray.
Little altar boy, please let me hear you pray.

Copyright © 1957 (Renewed 1985) by Famous Music LLC
International Copyright Secured   All Rights Reserved

The Little Boy That Santa Claus Forgot

Words and Music by Michael Carr, Tommy Connor and Jimmy Leach

Christmas comes but once a year for every girl and boy,
The laughter and the joy they find in each new toy.
I'll tell you of a little boy who lives across the way;
This little feller's Christmas is just another day.

He's the little boy that Santa Claus forgot,
And goodness knows he didn't want a lot.
He sent a note to Santa for some soldiers and a drum;
It broke his little heart when he found Santa hadn't come.

In the street he envies all those lucky boys,
Then wanders home to last year's broken toys.
I'm so sorry for that laddie,
He hasn't got a daddy,
The little boy that Santa Claus forgot.

Copyright © 1937 Shapiro, Bernstein & Co., Inc., New York
Copyright Renewed
International Copyright Secured   All Rights Reserved
Used by Permission

Little Saint Nick

Words and Music by Brian Wilson and Mike Love

Merry Christmas, Saint Nick.

Well, way up north where the air gets cold,
There's a tale about Christmas that you've all been told.
And a real famous cat all dressed up in red,
And he spends his whole year workin' out on his sled.

Refrain:
It's the little Saint Nick (little Saint Nick).
It's the little Saint Nick (little Saint Nick).

Just a little bobsled, we call it Old Saint Nick,
And she'll walk a toboggan with a four-speed stick.
She's a candy-apple red with a ski for a wheel,
And when Santa gives her gas, man, just watch her peel.

Refrain

Run, run, reindeer.
Run, run, reindeer.
Oh, run, run, reindeer.
Run, run, reindeer.
He don't miss no one.

And haulin' through the snow at a fright'nin' speed
With a half a dozen deer with Rudy to lead.
He's gotta wear his goggles 'cause the snow really flies,
And he's cruisin' every pad with a little surprise.

Refrain

Copyright © 1963 IRVING MUSIC, INC.
Copyright Renewed
All Rights Reserved   Used by Permission

Lo, How a Rose E'er Blooming

15th Century German Carol
Translated by Theodore Baker
Music from *Alte Catholische Geistliche Kirchengesang*

Lo, how a rose e'er blooming
From tender stem hath sprung!
Of Jesse's lineage coming
As men of old have sung.
It came, a flow'ret bright,
Amid the cold of winter,
When half spent was the night.

Isaiah 'twas foretold it,
The Rose I have in mind,
With Mary we behold it,
The Virgin Mother kind.
To show God's love aright,
She bore to men a Savior,
When half spent was the night.

Copyright © 2002 by HAL LEONARD CORPORATION
International Copyright Secured   All Rights Reserved

A Marshmallow World

Words by Carl Sigman
Music by Peter De Rose

It's a marshmallow world in the winter
When the snow comes to cover the ground.
It's the time for play, it's a whipped cream day,
I wait for it the whole year round.

Those are marshmallow clouds being friendly,
In the arms of the evergreen trees.
And the sun is red like a pumpkin head,
It's shining so your nose won't freeze.

The world is your snowball; see how it grows.
That's how it goes, whenever it snows.
The world is your snowball: just for a song,
Get out and roll it along.

It's a yum-yummy world made for sweethearts,
Take a walk with your favorite girl.
It's a sugar date, what if spring is late?
In winter it's a marshmallow world.

Copyright © 1949, 1950 Shapiro, Bernstein & Co., Inc., New York
Copyright Renewed
International Copyright Secured All Rights Reserved
Used by Permission

(Everybody's Waitin' For)
The Man with the Bag

Words and Music by Harold Stanley, Irving Taylor and Dudley Brooks

Old Mister Kringle is soon gonna jingle
The bells that'll tingle all your troubles away.
Everybody's waitin' for the man with the bag,
'Cause Christmas is comin' again.

He's got a sleigh full; it's not gonna stay full.
He's got stuff to drop at every stop of the way.
Everybody's waitin' for the man with the bag,
'Cause Christmas is comin' again.

He'll be here
With the answer to the prayers that you made through the year.
You'll get yours
If you've done everything you should extra special good.

He'll make this December the one you'll remember.
The best and the merriest you ever did have.
Everybody's waitin' for the man with the bag,
Christmas is here again.

Old Mister Kringle is soon gonna jingle
The bells that'll tingle all your troubles away.
Everybody's waitin' for the man with the bag,
Christmas is here again.

© 1954 (Renewed) MORLEY MUSIC CO.
All Rights Reserved

He's got a sleigh full; it's not gonna stay full.
He's got stuff to drop at every stop of the way.
Everybody's waitin' for the man with the bag,
Christmas is here again.

He'll be here
With the answer to the prayers that you made through the year.
You'll get yours
If you've done everything you should extra special good.

He'll make this December the one you'll remember.
The best and the merriest you ever did have.
Everybody's waitin', they're all congregatin',
Waiting for the man with the bag.

Spoken: Better watch out, now!

Mary Had a Baby

African-American Spiritual

Mary had a baby, oh Lord;
Mary had a baby, oh my Lord;
Mary had a baby, oh Lord;
The people keep a-coming and the train done gone.

What did she name him, oh Lord;
What did she name him, oh my Lord;
What did she name him, oh Lord;
The people keep a-coming and the train done gone.

She called him Jesus, oh Lord;
She called him Jesus, oh my Lord;
She called him Jesus, oh Lord;
The people keep a-coming and the train done gone.

Where was He born? Oh Lord;
Where was He born? Oh my Lord;
Where was He born? Oh Lord;
The people keep a-coming and the train done gone.

Born in a stable, oh Lord;
Born in a stable, oh my Lord;
Born in a stable, oh Lord;
The people keep a-coming and the train done gone.

Copyright © 2006 by HAL LEONARD CORPORATION
International Copyright Secured   All Rights Reserved

Where did they lay Him? Oh Lord;
Where did they lay Him? Oh my Lord;
Where did they lay Him? Oh Lord;
The people keep a-coming and the train done gone.

Laid Him in a manger, oh Lord;
Laid Him in a manger, oh my Lord;
Laid Him in a manger, oh Lord;
The people keep a-coming and the train done gone.

Mary's Little Boy

Words and Music by Massie Patterson and Sammy Heyward

Mary she had a little boy,
Mary she had a little boy,
Mary she had a little boy,
And they said His name was Wonderful.

Refrain:
He came down from heaven,
He came down from heaven,
He came down from heaven,
And they said His name was Wonderful.
Oh, yes, Wonderful, oh, yes, Counselor,
Wonderful, Counselor, He came down from heaven.

Soldiers looked for the little boy,
Soldiers looked for the little boy,
Soldiers looked for the little boy,
And they said His name was Wonderful.

Refrain

Wise men came running from the East,
Wise men came running from the East,
Wise men came running from the East,
And they said His name was Wonderful.

Refrain

TRO - © Copyright 1963 (Renewed) Ludlow Music, Inc., New York, NY
International Copyright Secured
All Rights Reserved Including Public Performance For Profit
Used by Permission

Mary's Little Boy Child

Words and Music by Jester Hairston

Long time ago in Bethlehem
So the holy Bible say,
Mary's boy child, Jesus Christ,
Was born on Christmas day.

Refrain:
Hark now hear the angels sing,
New King's born today,
And man will live forevermore
Because of Christmas day.

While shepherds watched their flocks by night
They saw a bright, new shining star
Heard a choir from Heaven sing.
The music came from afar.

Refrain

Now Joseph and his wife, Mary
Came to Bethlehem that night.
They found no place to bear her child,
Not a single room was in sight.

Refrain

Copyright © 1956 by Schumann Music
Copyright Renewed
International Copyright Secured   All Rights Reserved

Mele Kalikimaka

Words and Music by Alex Anderson

"Jingle Bells" upon steel guitar;
Through the palms we see the same bright star.

Mele Kalikimaka is the thing to say
On a bright Hawaiian Christmas day.
That's the island greeting that we send to you,
From the land where palm trees sway.
Here we know that Christmas will be green and bright.
The sun will shine by day, and all the stars at night.
Mele Kalikimaka is Hawaii's way
To say Merry Christmas to you.

Copyright © 1949 Lovely Hula Hands Music LLC
Copyright Renewed
All Rights Controlled and Administered by Lichelle Music Company
All Rights Reserved   Used by Permission

The Merry Christmas Polka

Words by Paul Francis Webster
Music by Sonny Burke

They're tuning up the fiddles now,
The fiddles now, the fiddles now,
There's wine to warm the middles now
And set your head awhirl.

Around and round the room we go,
The room we go, the room we go,
Around and round the room we go,
So get yourself a girl.

Now every heart will start to tingle,
When sleigh bells jingle on Santa's sleigh,
Together we will greet Kris Kringle
And another Christmas day.

Refrain:
Come on and dance the merry Christmas polka,
Let everyone be happy and gay.
Oh, it's the time to be jolly and deck the halls with holly,
So let's have a jolly holiday!

Come on and dance the merry Christmas polka,
Another joyous season has begun.
Roll out the yuletide barrels and sing out the carols,
A merry Christmas everyone!

Refrain

Copyright © 1949 by Alamo Music, Inc.
Copyright Renewed, Assigned to Chappell & Co. and Webster Music Co.
International Copyright Secured   All Rights Reserved

Merry Christmas, Darling

Words and Music by Richard Carpenter and Frank Pooler

Greeting cards have all been sent,
The Christmas rush is through,
But I still have one more wish to make,
A special one for you.

Merry Christmas, darling,
We're apart, that's true;
But I can dream and in my dreams,
I'm Christmas-ing with you.

Holidays are joyful,
There's always something new.
But every day's a holiday
When I'm near to you.

Copyright © 1970 IRVING MUSIC, INC.
Copyright Renewed
All Rights Reserved. Used by Permission

Refrain:
The lights on my tree
I wish you could see,
I wish it every day.
The logs on the fire
Fill me with desire
To see you and to say
That I wish you a merry Christmas,
Happy New Year too.
I've just one wish on this Christmas Eve;
I wish I were with you.

Refrain

I wish I were with you.
Merry Christmas, darling.

Merry, Merry Christmas, Baby

Words and Music by Margo Sylvia and Gilbert Lopez

Merry, merry Christmas, baby,
Although you're with somebody new,
Thought I'd send a card to say
That I wish this holiday
Would find me beside you.

Merry, merry Christmas baby,
And a happy New Year too.
It was Christmas Eve we met,
A holiday I can't forget,
'Cause that's when we fell in love.

I still remember the gifts we gave to each other.
This love I hold within my heart
Still grows, though we're apart.

Have a Merry Christmas, baby,
And a happy New Year too.
I am hoping that you'll find
A love as true as mine.
Merry, merry Christmas, baby.

Copyright © 1988 by Arc Music Corporation (BMI)
International Copyright Secured   All Rights Reserved
Used by Permission

A Merry, Merry Christmas to You

Music and Lyrics by Johnny Marks

Merry, merry, merry, merry, merry Christmas to you.
May each day be very, very happy all the year through.

Around the world you'll see the things the Christmas spirit can do.
Bells will be ringing with everyone singing a merry Christmas to you!

Joyeux Noël, Buonne Natale, Felize Navidad.
In every land there's a way of saying what we want to say.

Oh! Merry, merry, merry, merry, merry Christmas to you.
May each day be very, very happy all the year through.

Around the world you'll see the things the Christmas spirit can do.
Bells will be ringing with everyone singing a merry Christmas,
A Merry Christmas, a Merry Christmas to you!

Copyright © 1959 (Renewed 1987) St. Nicholas Music Inc., 1619 Broadway, New York, New York 10019
All Rights Reserved

Miss You Most
at Christmas Time

Words and Music by Mariah Carey and Walter Afanasieff

The fire is burning, the room's all aglow,
Outside the December wind blows.
Away in the distance
The carolers sing in the snow.

Everybody's laughing,
The world is celebrating
And everyone's so happy
Except for me tonight.

Because I miss you most at Christmas time
And I can't get you, get you off my mind.
Every other season comes along and I'm alright.
But then I miss you most at Christmas time.

Ooh, yeah, I gaze out the window this cold winter's night
At all of the twinkling lights,
Alone in the darkness,
Remembering when you were mine.

Everybody's smiling,
The whole world is rejoicing
And everyone's embracing
Except for you and I.

Copyright © 1994 Sony/ATV Tunes LLC, Wallyworld Music and Rye Songs
All Rights for Sony/ATV Tunes LLC and Wallyworld Music Administered by Sony/ATV Music Publishing,
    8 Music Square West, Nashville, TN 37203
All Rights for Rye Songs Controlled and Administered by Songs Of Universal, Inc.
International Copyright Secured   All Rights Reserved

Baby I miss you most at Christmas time
And I can't get you, get you off my mind.
Every other season comes along and I'm alright.
But then I miss you most at Christmas time.

Oh, in the springtime those memories start to fade
With the April rain.
Through the summer days till autumn's leaves are gone,
I get by without you till the snow begins to fall

And then I miss you most at Christmas time
And I can't get you, no-no-no-no, get you off my mind.
Every other season comes along and I'm all right.
But then I miss you most at Christmas time.

Mister Santa

Words and Music by Pat Ballard

Mister Santa, bring me some toys,
Bring Merry Christmas to all girls and boys.
And every night I'll go to bed singing
And dream about the presents you'll be bringing.
Santa, promise me, please,
Give every reindeer a hug and a squeeze.
I'll be good, as good as can be,
Mister Santa, don't forget me.

Mister Santa, dear old Saint Nick,
Be awful careful and please don't get sick.
Put on your coat when breezes are blowin',
And when you cross the street, look where you're goin'.
Santa, we (I) love you so,
We (I) hope you never get lost in the snow.
Take your time when you unpack,
Mister Santa, don't hurry back.

Mister Santa, we've been so good,
We've washed the dishes and done what we should.
Made up the beds and scrubbed up our toesies,
We've used Kleenex when we've blown our nosies.
Santa, look at our ears,
They're clean as whistles, we're sharper than shears.
Now we've put you on the spot,
Mister Santa, bring us a lot.

© 1954, 1955 (Renewed) EDWIN H. MORRIS & COMPANY, A Division of MPL Music Publishing, Inc.
All Rights Reserved

Mistletoe and Holly

Words and Music by Frank Sinatra, Dok Stanford and Henry W. Sanicola

Oh, by gosh, by golly,
It's time for mistletoe and holly,
Tasty pheasants, Christmas presents,
Countrysides covered with snow.

Oh, by gosh, by jingle,
It's time for carols and Kris Kringle,
Overeating, merry greetings
From relatives you don't know.

Then comes that big night,
Giving the tree the trim,
You'll hear voices by starlight
Singing a yuletide hymn.

Oh, by gosh, by golly,
It's time for mistletoe and holly,
Fancy ties and granny's pies
And folks stealin' a kiss or two
As they whisper "Merry Christmas to you."

Copyright © 1957 Barton Music Corp.
Copyright Renewed and Assigned to Sergeant Music Co. and Barton Music Corp.
All Rights on behalf of Sergeant Music Co. Administered by WB Music Corp.
All Rights Reserved   Used by Permission

The Most Wonderful Day of the Year

Music and Lyrics by Johnny Marks

We're on the island of Misfit Toys,
Here we don't want to stay.
We want to travel with Santa Claus,
In his magic sleigh.

Refrain:
A packful of toys means a sackful of joys
For millions of girls and for millions of boys
When Christmas day is here,
The most wonderful day of the year!

A jack-in-the-box waits for children to shout,
"Wake up, don't you know that it's time to come out!"
When Christmas day is here,
The most wonderful day of the year!

Toys galore, scattered on the floor,
There's no room for more,
And it's all because of Santa Claus!

A scooter for Jimmy, a dolly for Sue,
The kind that will even say "How do ya do!"
When Christmas day is here,
The most wonderful day of the year.

Copyright © 1964 (Renewed 1992) St. Nicholas Music Inc., 1619 Broadway, New York, New York 10019
All Rights Reserved

Refrain

It won't seem like Christmas till Dad gets his tie,
"It's just what I wanted" is his yearly cry.
When Christmas day is here,
The most wonderful day of the year.

Spirits gay, everyone will say, "Happy holiday!"
And the best to you the whole year through.
An electric train hidden high on the shelf
That Daddy gives David but then runs himself.

When Christmas day is here,
The most wonderful, wonderful, wonderful, wonderful,
Wonderful day of the year.

The Most Wonderful Time of the Year

Words and Music by Eddie Pola and George Wyle

It's the most wonderful time of the year,
With the kids jingle belling and everyone telling,
"You be of good cheer."
It's the most wonderful time of the year.

It's the hap-happiest season of all,
With those holiday greetings and gay happy meetings
When friends come to call.
It's the hap-happiest season of all.

There'll be parties for hosting,
Marshmallows for toasting,
And caroling out in the snow.
There'll be scary ghost stories
And tales of the glories
Of Christmases long, long ago.

It's the most wonderful time of the year.
There'll be much mistletoe-ing, and hearts will be glowing
When loved ones are near.
It's the most wonderful time of the year.

It's the most wonderful time of the year.
There'll be much mistletoe-ing, and hearts will be glowing
When loved ones are near.
It's the most wonderful time,
It's the most wonderful time,
It's the most wonderful time of the year.

Copyright © 1963 Barnaby Music Corp.
Copyright Renewed 1991
International Copyright Secured   All Rights Reserved

My Favorite Things

Lyrics by Oscar Hammerstein II
Music by Richard Rodgers

from *The Sound of Music*

Raindrops on roses and whiskers on kittens.
Bright copper kettles and warm woolen mittens.
Brown paper packages tied up with strings,
These are a few of my favorite things.

Cream-colored ponies and crisp apple strudels,
Doorbells and sleigh-bells and schnitzel with noodles,
Wild geese that fly with the moon on their wings,
These are a few of my favorite things.

Girls in white dresses with blue satin sashes,
Snowflakes that stay on my nose and eyelashes,
Silver white winters that melt into springs,
These are a few of my favorites things.

When the dog bites,
When the bee stings,
When I'm feeling sad,
I simply remember my favorite things
And then I don't feel so bad!

Copyright © 1959 by Richard Rodgers and Oscar Hammerstein II
Copyright Renewed
WILLIAMSON MUSIC owner of publication and allied rights throughout the world
International Copyright Secured   All Rights Reserved

My Only Wish This Year

Words and Music by Brian Kierulf and Joshua Schwartz

Last night I took a walk in the snow.
Couples holding hands; places to go.
Seems like everyone but me is in love.
Santa, can you hear me?

I signed my letter that I sealed with a kiss.
I sent it off, it just said this:
I know exactly what I want this year.
Santa, can you hear me?

I want my baby, baby, yeah.
I want someone to love me, someone to hold me.
Maybe, maybe, yeah,
He'll be all I hope in a big red bow.

Refrain:
Santa can you hear me?
I have been so good this year.
And all I want is one thing;
Tell me my true love is here.
He's all I want, just for me,
Underneath my Christmas tree.
I'll be waiting here.
Santa, that's my only wish this year.

Christmas Eve, I just can't sleep.
Would I be wrong for taking a peek?
'Cause I heard that you're coming to town.
Santa, can you hear me?

Copyright © 2000 by Zomba Enterprises, Inc., Kierulf Songs and Mugsy Boy Publishing
All Rights Administered by Zomba Enterprises, Inc.
International Copyright Secured   All Rights Reserved

I really hope that you are on your way
With something special for me in your sleigh.
Oh, please make my wish come true.
Santa, can you hear me?

I want my baby, baby, yeah.
I want someone to love me, someone to hold me.
Maybe, maybe, yeah,
We'll be all alone under the mistletoe.

Refrain

I hope my letter reaches you in time.
Bring me love I can call all mine.
'Cause I have been so good, so good this year.
Can't be alone under mistletoe;
He's all I want in a big red bow.

Refrain

Well, he's all I want, just for me,
Underneath my Christmas tree
I'll be waiting here.
Santa that's my only wish this year.
Santa that's my only wish this year.

The Night Before Christmas Song

Music by Johnny Marks
Lyrics adapted by Johnny Marks from Clement Moore's Poem

'Twas the night before Christmas and all through the house,
Not a creature was stirring, not even a mouse.
All the stockings were hung by the chimney with care,
In the hope that Saint Nicholas soon would be there.
Then what to my wondering eyes should appear,
A miniature sleigh and eight tiny reindeer,
A little old driver so lively and quick,
I knew in a moment it must be Saint Nick.
And more rapid than eagles his reindeer all came,
As he shouted, "On Dasher" and each reindeer's name.

And so up to the housetop the reindeer soon flew,
With the sleigh full of toys and Saint Nicholas too.
Down the chimney he came with a leap and a bound.
He was dressed all in fur and his belly was round.
He spoke not a word but went straight to his work,
And filled all the stockings, then turned with a jerk,
And laying his finger aside of his nose,
Then giving a nod, up the chimney he rose.
But I heard him exclaim as he drove out of sight,
"Merry Christmas to all, and to all a good night!"

Copyright © 1952 (Renewed 1980) St. Nicholas Music Inc., 1619 Broadway, New York, New York 10019
All Rights Reserved

No Eye Had Seen

Words by Amy Grant
Music by Michael W. Smith

Note: The song is a duet. The female lines are in parentheses. The parts are sung simultaneously.

No eye had seen, no ear had heard
'Til hosts on high proclaimed the birth.
And heav'n brought down its only Child,
(Quietly, with no one watching,
From the womb of perfect peace,)
The Son of Man, the world reconciled.
(Wellspring of the joy delivered
Into earthly destiny.)

(And song broke forth, angelic strain,
And none could help but sing the name.)
"Kyrie eleison," we sing, glory to the newborn King!)
Emmanuel! Emmanuel!
(Mortal and immortal voices, endless praises echoing!)
Emmanuel! Emmanuel!

Both: Emmanuel! Emmanuel!

Copyright © 1989 Sony/ATV Tunes LLC and Age To Age Music, Inc.
All Rights on behalf of Sony/ATV Tunes LLC Administered by Sony/ATV Music Publishing, 8 Music Square West, Nashville, TN 37203
All Rights on behalf of Age To Age Music, Inc. Administered by The Loving Company
International Copyright Secured   All Rights Reserved

Noel! Noel!

French-English Carol

Noel! Noel! Good news I tell,
And eke a wonder story:
A virgin mild hath borne a Child–
Jesus, the King of glory.

Copyright © 2006 by HAL LEONARD CORPORATION
International Copyright Secured   All Rights Reserved

Noel Nouvelet

Traditional French Carol

Christmas comes again,
Oh, sing we all Noel!
Glory be to God,
Now let our praises swell!

Refrain:
Sing we Noel
For Christ the newborn King, Noel.
Christmas comes again,
Oh, sing we all Noel.

Angels did proclaim,
Oh, shepherds come and see,
Born in Bethlehem
A blessed Lamb for thee.

Refrain

In the manger bare
The shepherds found the child,
Joseph stood well there
With Mary, Mother mild.

Refrain

Copyright © 2006 by HAL LEONARD CORPORATION
International Copyright Secured   All Rights Reserved

Nuttin' for Christmas

Words and Music by Roy Bennett and Sid Tepper

I broke my bat on Johnny's head;
Somebody snitched on me.
I hid a frog in sister's bed;
Somebody snitched on me.
I spilled some ink on Mommy's rug,
I made Tommy eat a bug,
Bought some gum with a penny slug;
Somebody snitched on me.

Refrain:
Oh, I'm gettin' nuttin' for Christmas.
Mommy and Daddy are mad.
I'm gettin' nuttin' for Christmas,
'Cause I ain't been nuttin' but bad.

I put a tack on teacher's chair;
Somebody snitched on me.
I tied a knot in Susie's hair;
Somebody snitched on me.
I did a dance on Mommy's plants,
Climbed a tree and tore my pants,
Filled the sugar bowl with ants;
Somebody snitched on me.

Refrain

Copyright © 1955 by Chappell & Co.
Copyright Renewed
International Copyright Secured   All Rights Reserved

I won't be seeing Santa Claus;
Somebody snitched on me.
He won't come visit me because
Somebody snitched on me.
Next year I'll be going straight,
Next year I'll be good, just wait,
I'd start now, but it's too late;
Somebody snitched on me.

Refrain

So you better be good, whatever you do,
'Cause if you're bad I'm warning you,
You'll get nuttin' for Christmas.

O Bethlehem

Traditional Spanish

O Bethlehem,
O'er you a brilliant star is shining,
O Bethlehem.

Heavenly choirs of angels bring
To the world glad news of an infant King;
Round you the hills and valleys are echoing!
O Bethlehem, O Bethlehem.

Copyright © 2006 by HAL LEONARD CORPORATION
International Copyright Secured   All Rights Reserved

O Christmas Tree

Traditional German Carol

O Christmas tree, o Christmas tree,
You stand in verdant beauty!
O Christmas tree, o Christmas tree,
You stand in verdant beauty!
Your boughs are green in summer's glow,
And do not fade in winter's snow.
O Christmas tree, o Christmas tree,
You stand in verdant beauty!

O Christmas tree, o Christmas tree,
Much pleasure doth thou bring me!
O Christmas tree, o Christmas tree,
Much pleasure doth thou bring me!
For every year the Christmas tree
Brings to us all both joy and glee.
O Christmas tree, o Christmas tree,
Much pleasure doth thou bring me!

O Christmas tree, O Christmas tree,
Thy candles shine out brightly!
O Christmas tree, O Christmas tree,
Thy candles shine out brightly!
Each bough doth hold its tiny light
That makes each toy to sparkle bright.
O Christmas tree, O Christmas tree,
Thy candles shine out brightly!

Copyright © 2002 by HAL LEONARD CORPORATION
International Copyright Secured   All Rights Reserved

O Come, All Ye Faithful (Adeste Fideles)

Words and Music by John Francis Wade
Latin Words translated by Frederick Oakeley

O come, all ye faithful, joyful and triumphant,
O come ye, o come ye to Bethlehem.
Come and behold Him, born the King of angels.

Refrain:
O come, let us adore Him,
O come, let us adore Him,
O come, let us adore Him,
Christ the Lord.

Sing, choirs of angels, sing in exultation,
Sing, all ye citizens of heaven above.
Glory to God in the highest.

Refrain

Yea, Lord, we greet Thee, born this happy morning.
Jesus, to Thee be all glory giv'n.
Word of the Father, now in flesh appearing.

Refrain

Copyright © 2002 by HAL LEONARD CORPORATION
International Copyright Secured   All Rights Reserved

O Come, Little Children

Words by C. von Schmidt
Music by J.P.A. Schulz

O come, little children, from cot and from hall,
O come to the manger in Bethlehem's stall.
There meekly he lieth, the heavenly Child,
So poor and so humble, so sweet and so mild.

Now "Glory to God" sing the angels on high,
And "Peace upon earth" heav'nly voices reply.
Then come, little children, and join in the day
That gladdened the world on that first Christmas day.

Copyright © 2002 by HAL LEONARD CORPORATION
International Copyright Secured   All Rights Reserved

O Come, O Come, Emmanuel

Plainsong, 13th Century
Words translated by John M. Neale and Henry S. Coffin

O come, o come, Emmanuel,
And ransom captive Israel,
That mourns in lonely exile here
Until the Son of God appear.

Refrain:
Rejoice, rejoice!
Emmanuel shall come to Thee, o Israel!

O come, Thou Dayspring, come and cheer
Our spirits by Thine advent here;
Disperse the gloomy clouds of night,
And death's dark shadows put to flight

Refrain

O come, Thou Wisdom, from on high,
And order all things far and nigh;
To us the path of knowledge show,
And cause us in her ways to go.

Refrain

Copyright © 2002 by HAL LEONARD CORPORATION
International Copyright Secured   All Rights Reserved

O come, desire of nations, bind
All people in one heart and mind;
Bid envy, strife, and quarrels cease;
Fill the whole world with heaven's peace.

Refrain

O come, Thou Key of David, come,
And open wide our heav'nly home.
Make safe the way that leads on high,
And close the path to misery.

Refrain

O Holy Night

French Words by Placide Cappeau
English Words by John S. Dwight
Music by Adolphe Adam

O holy night, the stars are brightly shining,
It is the night of the dear Savior's birth;
Long lay the world in sin and error pining,
Till He appeared and the soul felt its worth.
A thrill of hope, the weary world rejoices,
For yonder breaks a new and glorious morn;
Fall on your knees! O, hear the angel voices!
O night divine, o night when Christ was born!
O night, o holy night, o night divine!

Truly He taught us to love one another,
His law is love, and His gospel is peace;
Chains shall He break, for the slave is our brother,
And in His name all oppression shall cease.
Sweet hymns of joy in grateful chorus raise we,
Let all within us praise His holy name;
Christ is the Lord, o praise his name forever!
His pow'r and glory ever more proclaim!
His pow'r and glory ever more proclaim!

Copyright © 2002 by HAL LEONARD CORPORATION
International Copyright Secured   All Rights Reserved

O Thou Joyful

Traditional German Carol

O thou joyful, O thou wonderful
Grace revealing Christmastide!
Jesus came to win us from all sin within us;
Glorify, glorify the holy child.

O thou joyful, O thou wonderful
Love revealing Christmastide!
Loud hosannas singing and all praises bringing,
May the love, may the love with us abide.

O thou joyful, O thou wonderful
Peace revealing Christmastide!
Darkness disappeareth, God's own light now neareth,
Peace and joy, peace and joy to all betide.

Copyright © 2006 by HAL LEONARD CORPORATION
International Copyright Secured   All Rights Reserved

O Little Town of Bethlehem

Words by Phillips Brooks
Music by Lewis H. Redner

O little town of Bethlehem,
How still we see thee lie!
Above thy deep and dreamless sleep
The silent stars go by.
Yet in thy dark streets shineth
The everlasting light.
The hopes and fears of all the years
Are met in thee tonight.

For Christ is born of Mary,
And gathered all above,
While mortals sleep, the angels keep
Their watch of wond'ring love.
O morning stars, together
Proclaim the holy birth!
And praises sing to God the King,
And peace to men on earth!

Copyright © 2002 by HAL LEONARD CORPORATION
International Copyright Secured   All Rights Reserved

How silently, how silently
The wondrous gift is giv'n!
So God imparts to human hearts
The blessings of His heav'n.
No ear may hear His coming,
But in this world of sin,
Where meek souls will receive Him still,
The dear Christ enters in.

O holy Child of Bethlehem,
Descend to us, we pray;
Cast out our sin and enter in;
Be born in us today.
We hear the Christmas angels
The great glad tidings tell;
O come to us, abide with us,
Our Lord Emmanuel!

An Old Fashioned Christmas

Music and Lyrics by Johnny Marks

Let's have an old-fashioned Christmas
With holly on the door
And a bright Christmas tree for the whole family,
With presents all over the floor.
We'll sing the old fav'rite carols
When neighbors come to call.
Let's have an old-fashioned Christmas,
And a merry Christmas to all!

Copyright © 1952 (Renewed 1980) St. Nicholas Music Inc., 1619 Broadway, New York, New York 10019
All Rights Reserved

Old Toy Trains

Words and Music by Roger Miller

Old toy trains, little toy tracks,
Little toy drums comin' from a sack,
Carried by a man dressed in white and red.
Little boy, don't you think it's time you were in bed?
Close your eyes, listen to the skies,
All is calm, all is well;
Soon you'll hear Kris Kringle and the jingle bell

Bringin' little toy trains, little toy tracks,
Little toy drums comin' from a sack,
Carried by a man dressed in white and red.
Little boy, don't you think it's time you were in bed?
So close your eyes, listen to the skies,
All is calm, all is well;
Soon you'll hear Kris Kringle and the jingle bell

Bringin' little toy trains, little toy tracks,
Little toy drums comin' from a sack,
Carried by a man dressed in white and red.
Little boy, don't you think it's time you were in bed?

Copyright © 1967 Sony/ATV Songs LLC
Copyright Renewed
All Rights Administered by Sony/ATV Music Publishing, 8 Music Square West, Nashville, TN 37203
International Copyright Secured   All Rights Reserved

On Christmas Night

Sussex Carol

On Christmas night true Christians sing,
To hear the news the angels bring,
On Christmas night true Christians sing,
To hear the news the angels bring,
News of great joy and of great mirth,
Tidings of our dear Savior's birth.

The King of Kings to us is giv'n,
The Lord of earth and King of heav'n;
The King of Kings to us is giv'n,
The Lord of earth and King of heav'n;
Angels and men with joy may sing
Of blest Jesus, their newborn King.

So how on earth can men be sad,
When Jesus comes to make us glad?
So how on earth can men be sad,
When Jesus comes to make us glad?
From all our sins to set us free,
Buying for us our liberty.

From out of darkness we have light,
Which makes the Angels sing this night;
From out of darkness we have light,
Which makes the Angels sing this night:
"Glory to God, His peace to men,
And goodwill, evermore! Amen."

Copyright © 2002 by HAL LEONARD CORPORATION
International Copyright Secured   All Rights Reserved

Once in Royal David's City

Words by Cecil F. Alexander
Music by Henry J. Gauntlett

Once in royal David's city
Stood a lowly cattle shed,
Where a mother laid her Baby
In a manger for His bed.
Mary was that mother mild,
Jesus Christ her little child.

He came down to earth from heaven,
Who is God and Lord of all,
And His shelter was a stable,
And His cradle was a stall.
With the poor, and mean, and lowly,
Lived on earth our Savior holy.

Jesus is our childhood's pattern,
Day by day like us He grew;
He was little, weak and helpless,
Tears and smiles like us He knew.
And He feeleth for our sadness,
And He shareth in our gladness.

And our eyes at last shall see Him,
Through His own redeeming love,
For that child so dear and gentle
Is our Lord in heav'n above.
And He leads His children on
To the place where He is gone.

Copyright © 2002 by HAL LEONARD CORPORATION
International Copyright Secured   All Rights Reserved

One Bright Star

Words and Music by John Jarvis

Long long ago in a world dark and cold,
A night so still, winter's chill,
One bright star was shining.
On a bed made of hay in a manger He lay.
The shepherds came, they knew His name,
King of Kings. A brand new day,
They saw the light in the darkness.
It shines on love and tenderness,
Brings out the hope that's in all of us.
May it shine its light on you this Christmas night.

On this Christmas day, may that star light your way.
This Christmas Eve, I still believe that same star still shines on me.
I saw the light in the darkness.
It shines on love and tenderness,
Brings out the hope that's in all of us.
May it shine its light on you this Christmas night.
May it shine its light on you this Christmas night.

Copyright © 1985 Sony/ATV Songs LLC
All Rights Administered by Sony/ATV Music Publishing, 8 Music Square West, Nashville, TN 37203
International Copyright Secured   All Rights Reserved

Pat-A-Pan
(Willie, Take Your Little Drum)

Words and Music by Bernard de la Monnoye

Willie, take your little drum,
Robin, bring your whistle, come.
When we hear the fife and drum,
Tu-re-lu-re-lu, pat-a-pat-a-pan.
When we hear the fife and drum,
Christmas should be light and fun.

Thus the men of olden days
Gave the King of Kings their praise.
When they hear the fife and drum,
Tu-re-lu-re-lu, pat-a-pat-a-pan.
With the drums they sing and play,
Full of joy on Christmas day.

God and man are now become
Closely joined as fife and drum.
When we play the fife and drum,
Tu-re-lu-re-lu, pat-a-pat-a-pan.
When on fife and drum we play,
Dance and make the holiday.

Copyright © 2002 by HAL LEONARD CORPORATION
International Copyright Secured   All Rights Reserved

One for the Little Bitty Baby (Go Where I Send Thee)

Spiritual Arranged by Ronnie Gilbert, Lee Hays, Fred Hellerman and Pete Seeger

Children, go where I send thee!
How shall I send thee?
I'm a-gonna send you one by one;
One for the little bitty baby
That's born, born, born in Bethlehem.

Children, go where I send thee!
How shall I send thee?
I'm a gonna send you two by two;
Two for Paul and Silas,
One for the little bitty baby
That's born, born, born in Bethlehem.

Children, go where I send thee!
How shall I send thee?
I'm a-gonna send you three by three;
Three for the Hebrew children,
Two for Paul and Silas,
One for the little bitty baby
That's born, born, born in Bethlehem.

Children, go where I send thee!
How shall I send thee?
I'm a-gonna send you four by four;
Four for the four that stood at the door,
Three for the Hebrew children,
Two for Paul and Silas,
One for the little bitty baby
That's born, born, born in Bethlehem.

TRO - © Copyright 1951 (Renewed) Folkways Music Publishers, Inc., New York, NY
International Copyright Secured
All Rights Reserved Including Public Performance For Profit
Used by Permission

Children, go where I send thee!
How shall I send thee?
I'm a-gonna send you five by five;
Five for the gospel preachers,
Four for the four that stood at the door,
Three for the Hebrew children,
Two for Paul and Silas,
One for the little bitty baby
That's born, born, born in Bethlehem.

Children, go where I send thee!
How shall I send thee?
I'm a-gonna send you six by six;
Six for the six that never got fixed,
Five for the gospel preachers,
Four for the four that stood at the door,
Three for the Hebrew children,
Two for Paul and Silas,
One for the little bitty baby
That's born, born, born in Bethlehem.

Children, go where I send thee!
How shall I send thee?
I'm a-gonna send you seven by seven;
Seven for the seven that never got to heaven,
Six for the six that never got fixed,
Five for the gospel preachers,
Four for the four that stood at the door,
Three for the Hebrew children,
Two for Paul and Silas,
One for the little bitty baby
That's born, born, born in Bethlehem.

Children, go where I send thee!
How shall I send thee?
I'm a-gonna send you eight by eight;
Eight for the eight that stood at the gate,
Seven for the seven that never got to heaven,
Six for the six that never got fixed,
Five for the gospel preachers,
Four for the four that stood at the door,
Three for the Hebrew children,
Two for Paul and Silas,
One for the little bitty baby
That's born, born, born in Bethlehem.

Children, go where I send thee!
How shall I send thee?
I'm a-gonna send you nine by nine;
Nine for the nine all dressed so fine,
Eight for the eight that stood at the gate,
Seven for the seven that never got to heaven,
Six for the six that never got fixed,
Five for the gospel preachers,
Four for the four that stood at the door,
Three for the Hebrew children,
Two for Paul and Silas,
One for the little bitty baby
That's born, born, born in Bethlehem.

Children, go where I send thee!
How shall I send thee?
I'm a-gonna send you ten by ten;
Ten for the Ten Commandments,
Nine for the nine all dressed so fine,
Eight for the eight that stood at the gate,
Seven for the seven that never got to heaven,
Six for the six that never got fixed,
Five for the gospel preachers,
Four for the four that stood at the door,
Three for the Hebrew children,
Two for Paul and Silas,
One for the little bitty baby
That's born, born, born in Bethlehem.

One King

Words and Music by Jeff Borders, Gayla Borders and Lowell Alexander

Kings of earth on a course unknown, bearing gifts from afar;
Hoping, praying, following yonder star.
Silhouette of a caravan painted against the sky;
Wise men searching for the holy Child.

Refrain:
One king held the frankincense,
One king held the myrrh,
One king held the purest gold,
And one King held the hope of the world.

A star hangs over Bethlehem; a journey ends in the night.
Three kings, trembling behold the glorious sight.
Heaven's treasure, Emmanuel, drawing men to bow down;
Tiny baby, born to wear a crown.

Refrain

God rest ye merry, gentlemen, let nothing you dismay.
Remember Christ, our Savior was born on Christmas Day
To say us all from Satan's pow'r when we were gone astray.
Oh, tiny baby born to wear a crown.

Copyright © 1998, 1999 Sony/ATV Tunes LLC, Sony/ATV Songs LLC, Grayson Castle Songs, Bridge Building and
    Randy Cox Music, Inc.
All Rights on behalf of Sony/ATV Tunes LLC, Sony/ATV Songs LLC and Grayson Castle Songs Administered by
    Sony/ATV Music Publishing, 8 Music Square West, Nashville, TN 37203
All Rights on behalf of Bridge Building and Randy Cox Music, Inc. Administered by Brentwood-Benson Music
    Publishing, Inc.
International Copyright Secured   All Rights Reserved

One king held the frankincense,
One king held the myrrh,
One king held the purest gold,
One King held the hope of the world,
The hope of the world.

One king held the purest gold;
One King held the hope of the world.

Out of the East

Words and Music by Harry Noble

Out of the East there came riding, riding,
Three of the wisest of men,
Dust was their enemy blinding, blinding,
Even the wisest of them.
Wandering shepherds heard tell their story,
Told in the flickering firelight, tender light,
Ever bright Christmas night.
Far to the West was there shining, shining,
Blazing a star in the dawn;
Reverent wise men beheld it, saying
This night a Savior is born.

Into the West they went riding, riding,
Following after the star,
Over a quiet town shining, shining,
Lighting their way from afar.
Under its glory sat mother Mary,
Tenderly singing a lullabye,
Don't you cry lullaby.
Into the stable came riding, riding,
Three of the wisest of men;
Gifts did they bring for that babe in manger,
Gifts for the Savior of men.

Copyright © 1941 by The Boston Music Company
Copyright Renewed 1968
Renewal Copyright Assigned 1969 to Larry Spier, Inc., New York, NY
International Copyright Secured   All Rights Reserved

Low in a manger they found him, found him,
Bathed in the light of yon star,
Gold did they bring him and frankincense
And myrrh from a land that was far,
Shepherds crept in singing praises, praises,
Angels kept watch to be near to Him, dear to Him,
One with him, praising Him.
Into the East then went riding, riding,
Three of the wisest of men;
Found was the babe in a lowly manger,
Crowned was the Savior of men.

Please Come Home for Christmas

Words and Music by Charles Brown and Gene Redd

Bells will be ringing the sad, sad news,
Oh what a Christmas to have the blues!
My baby's gone, I have no friends
To wish me greetings once again.

Choirs will be singing "Silent Night,"
Christmas carols by candlelight.
Please come home for Christmas,
Please come home for Christmas;
If not for Christmas, by New Year's night.

Friends and relations send salutations
Sure as the star shine above.
For this is Christmas, yes, Christmas my dear,
It's the time of year to be with the one you love.

So won't you tell me you'll nevermore roam.
Christmas and New Year will find you home.
There'll be no more sorrow, no grief and pain
And I'll be happy, happy once again.

There'll be no more sorrow, no grief and pain
And I'll be happy, Christmas once again.

Copyright © 1960 by Fort Knox Music Inc. and Trio Music Company
Copyright Renewed
International Copyright Secured   All Rights Reserved
Used by Permission

Poor Little Jesus

Arranged by Ronnie Gilbert, Lee Hays, Fred Hellerman and Pete Seeger

It was poor little Jesus, yes, yes.
Born on Friday, yes, yes.
And they laid Him in a manger, yes, yes.

Refrain:
Wasn't that a pity and a shame, oh, Lord!
Wasn't that a pity and a shame!

It was poor little Jesus, yes, yes.
Child of Mary, yes, yes.
Didn't have no shelter, yes, yes.

Refrain

It was poor little Jesus, yes, yes.
They whipped Him up a mountain, yes, yes.
And they hung Him with a robber, yes, yes.

Refrain

He was born on Christmas, yes, yes.
He was born on Christmas, yes, yes.
Didn't have no cradle, yes, yes.

Refrain

TRO - © Copyright 1951 (Renewed) and 1952 (Renewed) Folkways Music Publishers, Inc., New York, NY
International Copyright Secured
All Rights Reserved Including Public Performance For Profit
Used by Permission

Precious Promise

Words and Music by Steven Curtis Chapman

Oh, what a precious promise,
Oh, what a gift of love;
An angel tells a virgin that
She's gonna have a son.
And though it's a precious promise,
She wonders how can this be?
What will the people say
And what if Joseph can't believe?
And her questions and her fears
Are met with an overwhelming joy
That God has chosen her.
Oh, what a precious promise;
Mary waits as heaven comes to earth.

Oh, what a precious promise,
Oh, what a gift of love.
Joseph makes his choice to do
What few men would have done:
To take Mary as his bride
When she's already carrying a child
That isn't his own.
Oh, what a precious promise;
Mary and the child will have a home.

© 1995 SPARROW SONG (BMI) and PEACH HILL SONGS (BMI)
Admin. by EMI CMG PUBLISHING
All Rights Reserved   Used by Permission

And shepherds stand on a hillside,
Their hearts racing with the news the angel told them.
A star's light fills up the dark sky
As the night of precious promise is unfolding.

Oh, what a precious promise,
Oh, what a gift of love.
The waiting now is over
And the time has fin'lly come
For the God who made this world
To roll back the curtain and unveil
His passion for the heart of man.
Oh, what a precious promise;
Lying in a manger in Bethlehem.
Oh, what a precious promise,
Lying in a manger in Bethlehem.

Pretty Paper

Words and Music by Willie Nelson

Crowded streets, busy feet hustle by him.
Downtown shoppers, Christmas is night.
There he sits all alone on the sidewalk.
Hoping that you won't pass him by.

Should you stop? Better not,
Much too busy. You're in a hurry.
My, how time does fly.
In the distance the ringing of laughter,
And in the midst of the laughter he cries.

Refrain:
Pretty paper, pretty ribbons of blue.
Wrap your presents to your darling from you.
Pretty pencils to write, "I love you."
Pretty paper, pretty ribbons of blue.

Repeat Refrain

Copyright © 1962 Sony/ATV Songs LLC
Copyright Renewed
All Rights Administered by Sony/ATV Music Publishing, 8 Music Square West, Nashville, TN 37203
International Copyright Secured   All Rights Reserved

Rockin' Around the Christmas Tree

Music and Lyrics by Johnny Marks

Rockin' around the Christmas tree
At the Christmas party hop.
Mistletoe hung where you can see,
Every couple tries to stop.

Rockin' around the Christmas tree,
Let the Christmas spirit ring.
Later we'll have some pun'kin pie
And we'll do some caroling.

You will get a sentimental feeling when you hear
Voices singing "Let's be jolly,
Deck the halls with boughs of holly!"

Rockin' around the Christmas tree.
Have a happy holiday.
Everyone dancing merrily
In the new old-fashioned way.

Copyright © 1958 (Renewed 1986) St. Nicholas Music Inc., 1619 Broadway, New York, New York 10019
All Rights Reserved

Rose of Bethlehem

Words and Music by Lowell Alexander

There's a Rose in Bethlehem
With a beauty quite divine,
Perfect in this world of sin
On this silent holy night.

There's a fragrance much like hope
That it sends upon the wind,
Reaching out to every soul
From a lowly manger's crib.

Refrain:
Oh, Rose of Bethlehem,
How lovely, pure and sweet,
Born to glorify the Father,
Born to wear the thorns for me.

There's a Rose in Bethlehem
Colored red like mercy's blood.
'Tis the flower of our faith;
'Tis the blossom of God's love.

Though its bloom is fresh with youth,
Surely what will be He knows,
For a tear of morning dew
Is rolling down the Rose.

Refrain Twice

Born to glorify the Father,
Born to wear the thorns for me.

© 1992 BIRDWING MUSIC (ASCAP)
Admin. by EMI CMG PUBLISHING
All Rights Reserved   Used by Permission

Rudolph the
Red-Nosed Reindeer

Music and Lyrics by Johnny Marks

You know Dasher and Dancer and Prancer and Vixen,
Comet and Cupid and Donner and Blitzen,
But do you recall
The most famous reindeer of all?

Rudolph, the red-nosed reindeer
Had a very shiny nose,
And, if you ever saw it,
You would even say it glows.
All of the other reindeer
Used to laugh and call him names,
They never let poor Rudolph
Join in any reindeer games.
Then one foggy Christmas Eve
Santa came to say,
"Rudolph, with your nose so bright,
Won't you guide my sleigh tonight?"
Then how the reindeer loved him
As they shouted out with glee:
"Rudolph, the red-nosed reindeer,
You'll go down in history!"

Copyright © 1949 (Renewed 1977) St. Nicholas Music Inc., 1619 Broadway, New York, New York 10019
All Rights Reserved

Santa Baby

By Joan Javits, Phil Springer and Tony Springer

Mister Claus, I feel as though I know ya,
So you won't mind if I should get familya, will ya?

Santa baby, slip a sable under the tree for me.
I've been an awful good girl, Santa baby,
So hurry down the chimney tonight.

Santa baby, a fifty-four convertible, too, light blue.
I'll wait up for you, dear Santa baby,
So hurry down the chimney tonight.

Think of all the fun I've missed.
Think of all the fellas that I haven't kissed.
Next year I could be just as good
If you check off my Christmas list.

Santa baby, I want a yacht and really that's not a lot.
Been an angel all year, Santa baby,
So hurry down the chimney tonight.

Santa baby, one little thing I really do need,
The deed to a platinum mine, Santa honey,
So hurry down the chimney tonight.

Copyright © 1953 Trinity Music, Inc.
Copyright Renewed 1981 and Controlled in the U.S. by Philip Springer
Copyright Controlled for the world outside the U.S. by Alley Music Corp. and Trio Music Company
International Copyright Secured   All Rights Reserved

Santa cutie, and fill my stocking with a duplex and cheques.
Sign your X on the line, Santa cutie,
And hurry down the chimney tonight.

Come and trim my Christmas tree
With some decorations bought at Tiffany.
I really do believe in you.
Let's see if you believe in me.

Santa baby, forgot to mention one little thing,a ring!
I don't mean a phone, Santa baby,
So hurry down the chimney tonight.

Santa, Bring My Baby Back (To Me)

Words and Music by Claude DeMetruis and Aaron Schroeder

Don't need a lot of presents
To make my Christmas bright.
I just need my baby's arms
Wound around me tight.

Refrain:
Oh, Santa, hear my plea.
Santa, bring my baby back to me.

The Christmas tree is ready,
The candles all aglow,
But with my baby far away
What good is mistletoe?

Refrain

Please make those reindeer hurry;
The time is drawin' near.
It sure won't seem like Christmas
Unless my baby's here.

Don't fill my sock with candy,
No bright and shiny toy.
You wanna make me happy
And fill my heart with joy,

Then, Santa, hear my plea.
Santa, bring my baby back to me.

Copyright © 1957 by Gladys Music, Inc.
Copyright Renewed and Assigned to Gladys Music and Rachel's Own Music
All Rights for Gladys Music Administered by Cherry Lane Music Publishing Company, Inc. and Chrysalis Music
All Rights for Rachel's Own Music Administered by A. Schroeder International LLC
International Copyright Secured   All Rights Reserved

Santa Claus Is Comin' to Town

Words by Haven Gillespie
Music by J. Fred Coots

You better watch out, you better not cry,
Better not pout, I'm telling you why:
Santa Claus is comin' to town.

He's making a list and checking it twice,
Gonna find out who's naughty and nice.
Santa Claus is comin' to town.

He sees you when you're sleepin'.
He knows when you're awake.
He knows if you've been bad or good,
So be good for goodness sake.

Oh! You better watch out, you better not cry,
Better not pout, I'm telling you why:
Santa Claus is comin' to town.

© 1934 (Renewed 1962) EMI FEIST CATALOG INC.
Rights for the Extended Renewal Term in the United States Controlled by HAVEN GILLESPIE MUSIC and
    EMI FEIST CATALOG INC.
All Rights for HAVEN GILLESPIE MUSIC Administered by THE SONGWRITERS GUILD OF AMERICA
All Rights outside the United States Controlled by EMI FEIST CATALOG INC. (Publishing) and WARNER BROS.
    PUBLICATIONS U.S. INC. (Print)
All Rights Reserved   Used by Permission

The Santa Claus Parade

Music and Lyrics by Johnny Marks

There's a happy celebration
In each town across the nation
At the Santa Claus Parade.
All the grown-ups and the kiddies
In the towns and in the cities
Love the Santa Claus Parade.
Dasher, Dancer, Prancer, Vixen,
Comet, Cupid, Donner, Blitzen,
Rudolph leads the whole brigade.
When you hear all the cheering
You will see Santa nearing
At the Santa Claus Parade.

Clowns come tumbling all along the way
As every band begins to play:
"To all a happy holiday."
And when you see the presents loaded in the sleigh,
You'll know that Christmas isn't very far away.

Repeat Verse 1

Copyright © 1960 (Renewed 1988) St. Nicholas Music Inc., 1619 Broadway, New York, New York 10019
All Rights Reserved

Shake Me I Rattle
(Squeeze Me I Cry)

Words and Music by Hal Hackady and Charles Naylor

I was passing by a toy shop on the corner of the square,
Where a little girl was looking in the window there.
She was looking at a dolly in a dress of rosy red.
And around the pretty dolly hung a little sign that said:

Refrain:
Shake me I rattle, squeeze me I cry
As I stood there beside her I could hear her sigh.
Shake me I rattle, squeeze me I cry.
Please take me home and love me.

I recalled another toy shop on a square so long ago
Where I saw a little dolly that I wanted so.
I remembered, I remembered how I longed to make it mine.
And around that other dolly hung another little sign:

Refrain

It was late and snow was following as the shoppers hurried by,
Past the girlie at the window with her little head held high.
They were closing up the toy shop as I hurried through the door.
Just in time to buy the dolly that her heart was longing for.

Refrain

Copyright © 1957 (Renewed) by Regent Music Corporation (BMI)
International Copyright Secured   All Rights Reserved
Used by Permission

Share Love

Words and Music by Nathan Morris

It's that time of the year again
For you to share
All the love that you have
With every woman and every man,
To share love.

Christmas Day is here
And the Lord has brought us near
To share love with your family
And thank God for allowing you to see that
Christmas is the time to share
With the one you love.
Share good things, joy, and glad tidings.
Share love.
Giving all you have this day
Lets the world know that you care
And you will be there to share love.

Families all around,
Children are happy with what they found,
Giving things on this day
And thanking our God,
For teaching us the way to share love.

Copyright © 1993 by Vanderpool Publishing and Ensign Music LLC
International Copyright Secured   All Rights Reserved

As the snow is falling down,
Presents unwrapped underneath the tree
Bringing tidings of great joy
To every little girl and boy.
You know Christmas is the time to share
With the one you love.
Share good things, joy, and glad tidings.
Share love.
Giving all you have this day
Lets the world know that you care
And you will be there to share love.

Now the true meaning of Christmas
Is falling on your knees
And thanking the Lord
For what He's done,
Giving the world His only Son.

Repeat and Fade:
Christmas is the time to share
With the one you love.
Share good things, joy, and glad tidings.
Share love.
Giving all you have this day
Lets the world know that you care
And you will be there to share love.
Oh, ooh, let Him in.

Shepherds, Shake Off Your Drowsy Sleep

Traditional French Carol

Shepherds, shake off your drowsy sleep;
Rise and leave your silly sheep.
Angels from Heav'n around are singing,
Tidings of great joy are bringing.

Refrain:
Shepherds, the chorus come and swell!
Sing Noel, O sing Noel!

See how the flow'rs all burst anew,
Thinking snow is summer dew.
See how the stars afresh are glowing,
All their brightest beams bestowing.

Refrain

Shepherds, then up and quick away!
Seeking the Babe ere break of day.
He is the hope of every nation;
All in Him shall find salvation.

Refrain

Copyright © 2006 by HAL LEONARD CORPORATION
International Copyright Secured   All Rights Reserved

Shout the Glad Tidings

Traditional

Shout the glad tidings, exultingly sing;
Jerusalem triumphs, Messiah is King!

Zion, the marvelous story be telling;
The Son of the Highest, how lowly His birth!
The brightest archangel in glory excelling,
He stoops to redeem thee, He reigns upon earth.

Shout the glad tidings, exultingly sing;
Jerusalem triumphs, Messiah is King!

Copyright © 2006 by HAL LEONARD CORPORATION
International Copyright Secured   All Rights Reserved

Silent Night

Words by Joseph Mohr
Translated by John F. Young
Music by Franz X. Gruber

Silent night, holy night!
All is calm, all is bright.
Round yon Virgin Mother and Child.
Holy Infant so tender and mild,
Sleep in heavenly peace,
Sleep in heavenly peace.

Silent night, holy night!
Shepherds quake at the sight.
Glories stream from heaven afar,
Heavenly hosts sing Alleluia,
Christ the Savior is born!
Christ the Savior is born.

Silent night, holy night!
Son of God, love's pure light.
Radiant beams from thy holy face
With the dawn of redeeming grace,
Jesus, Lord, at Thy birth.
Jesus, Lord, at Thy birth.

Copyright © 2002 by HAL LEONARD CORPORATION
International Copyright Secured   All Rights Reserved

Silver and Gold

Music and Lyrics by Johnny Marks

Silver and gold, silver and gold,
Everyone wishes for silver and gold,
How do you measure its worth?
Just by the pleasure it gives here on earth?

Silver and gold, silver and gold,
Mean so much more when I see
Silver and gold decorations
On every Christmas tree.

Copyright © 1964 (Renewed 1992) St. Nicholas Music Inc., 1619 Broadway, New York, New York 10019
All Rights Reserved

Silver Bells

Words and Music by Jay Livingston and Ray Evans

from the Paramount Picture *The Lemon Drop Kid*

Christmas makes you feel emotional.
It may bring parties or thoughts devotional.
Whatever happens or what may be,
Here is what Christmastime means to me.

City sidewalks, busy sidewalks,
Dressed in holiday style;
In the air there's a feeling of Christmas.
Children laughing, people passing,
Meeting smile after smile,
And on every street corner you hear:

Refrain:
Silver bells, silver bells,
It's Christmastime in the city.
Ring-a-ling, hear them ring,
Soon it will be Christmas day.

Strings of street lights, even stoplights
Blink a bright red and green
As the shoppers rush home with their treasures.
Hear the snow crunch, see the kids bunch,
This is Santa's big scene,
And above all this bustle you hear:

Refrain

Copyright © 1950 (Renewed 1977) by Paramount Music Corporation
International Copyright Secured   All Rights Reserved

Sing We Now of Christmas

Traditional

Sing we now of Christmas,
Noel sing we here.
Hear our grateful praises
To the Babe so dear.

Sing we Noel!
The King is born. Noel!
Sing we now of Christmas,
Sing we now Noel.

From the eastern country
Came the kings afar,
Bearing gifts to Bethl'hem,
Guided by a star

Sing we Noel!
The King is born. Noel!
Sing we now of Christmas,
Sing we now Noel.

Copyright © 2006 by HAL LEONARD CORPORATION
International Copyright Secured   All Rights Reserved

Sleep, Holy Babe

Words by Edward Caswell
Music by J.B. Dykes

Sleep, Holy Babe,
Upon Thy mother's breast.
Great Lord of earth and sea and sky,
How sweet it is to see Thee lie
In such a place of rest,
In such a place of rest!

Sleep, Holy Babe,
Thine angel's watch around,
All bending low with folded wings
Before the incarnate King of kings
In rev'rent awe profound,
In rev'rent awe profound.

Copyright © 2006 by HAL LEONARD CORPORATION
International Copyright Secured   All Rights Reserved

The Snow Lay on the Ground

Traditional Irish Carol

The snow lay on the ground, the star shone bright,
When Christ our Lord was born on Christmas night.
Venite adoremus Dominum;
Venite adoremus Dominum.

Refrain:
Venite adoremus Dominum;
Venite adoremus Dominum.

'Twas Mary, Virgin pure, of holy Anne,
That brought into this world the God made man.
She laid Him in a stall at Bethlehem,
The ass and oxen share the night with them.

Refrain

Saint Joseph, too, was by to tend the Child;
To guard Him and protect His Mother mild;
The Angels hovered round and sang this song:
Venite adoremus Dominum.

Refrain

Copyright © 2002 by HAL LEONARD CORPORATION
International Copyright Secured   All Rights Reserved

Snowfall

Lyrics by Ruth Thornhill
Music by Claude Thornhill

Snowfall, softly, gently drift down.
Snowflakes whisper 'neath my window.
Cov'ring trees misty white,
Velvet breeze 'round my doorstep.
Gently, softly, silent snowfall!

Copyright © 1941, 1968 by Chappell & Co.
Copyright Renewed
International Copyright Secured   All Rights Reserved

Some Children See Him

Lyric by Wihla Hutson
Music by Alfred Burt

Some children see Him lily white,
The Baby Jesus born this night.
Some children see Him lily white,
With tresses soft and fair.

Some children see Him bronzed and brown,
The Lord of heav'n to earth come down;
Some children see Him bronzed and brown,
With dark and heavy hair.

Some children see Him almond-eyed,
This Savior whom we kneel beside,
Some children see Him almond-eyed,
With skin of yellow hue.

Some children see Him dark as they,
Sweet Mary's Son to whom we pray;
Some children see Him dark as they,
And, ah, they love Him too!

The children in each diff'rent place
Will see the Baby Jesus' face
Like theirs, but bright with heav'nly grace,
And filled with holy light.

O lay aside each earthly thing,
And with thy heart as offering,
Come worship now the Infant King,
'Tis love that's born tonight!

TRO – © Copyright 1954 (Renewed) and 1957 (Renewed) Hollis Music, Inc., New York, NY
International Copyright Secured
All Rights Reserved Including Public Performance For Profit
Used by Permission

Somewhere in My Memory

Words by Leslie Bricusse
Music by John Williams

from the Twentieth Century Fox Motion Picture *Home Alone*

Candles in the window,
Shadows painting the ceiling,
Gazing at the fire glow,
Feeling that "gingerbread" feeling.
Precious moments, special people,
Happy faces I can see.

Somewhere in my mem'ry,
Christmas joys all around me,
Living in my mem'ry,
All of the music, all of the magic,
All of the fam'ly home here with me.

Copyright © 1990, 1991 Fox Film Music Corporation and John Hughes Songs
All Rights Reserved   Used by Permission

The Star

Words and Music by Peter McCann

Just another homeless family
Hoping for a stranger's charity,
Just one night in one safe place to stay,
Underneath the star so far away.

She carried everything they had and more,
The little one the world was waiting for.
And somewhere in the night her child was born
Into every heart so tired and torn.

Refrain:
And the light shining from that star
Will show you who you are.
And His light shining with its might
Will lead you through the darkest night.

They couldn't find a room for Him back then,
But he found a place in the hearts of men.
The hope that all the world would come to know,
Born beneath the star so long ago.

Refrain

Just another homeless family,
Hoping for a stranger's charity,
Just one night in one safe place to stay,
Underneath the star so far away.

© 1993 EMI APRIL MUSIC INC. and NEW AND USED MUSIC
All Rights Controlled and Administered by EMI APRIL MUSIC INC.
All Rights Reserved   International Copyright Secured   Used by Permission

Special Gift

Words and Music by Myron Davis and Stanley Brown

You are my special gift.
I have searched everywhere;
Nothing can compare.
Gift.

You are my special gift.
I have searched everywhere;
Nothing else can compare.
Gift.

As the lights on the tree
Set the mood on Christmas Eve.
Anticipating,
Girl, you know you got me waiting.

Wrapped in such a pretty bow.
What's inside? I gotta know.
I can hardly sleep, baby.
'Cause I know there's something there.

You are my special gift.
I have searched everywhere;
Nothing can compare.
Gift.

You are my special gift.
I have searched everywhere;
Nothing else can compare.
Gift.

© 1996 EMI BLACKWOOD MUSIC INC., M DOUBLE MUSIC and STAN BROWN MUSIC
All Rights for M DOUBLE MUSIC Controlled and Administered by EMI BLACKWOOD MUSIC INC.
All Rights Reserved   International Copyright Secured   Used by Permission

I hear sleigh bells ringing;
In the streets everybody's singing.
Sharing the love, sharing the joy.
If they only knew what I'm dreaming of.

As I look under the tree
I know there's something there for me.
Girl, I need it, gotta have it.
You know I want it, babe.

As I sit here by the fire,
I know that you're my heart's desire.
And the very thought of you, girl,
Seems to make my dreams come true.

Every night and day I'll wait,
Hoping soon I'll see your face.
Girl, I want you, babe.
I need you, babe. Gotta have.

You are my special gift.
I have searched everywhere;
Nothing can compare.
Gift.

You are my special gift.
I have searched everywhere;
Nothing else can compare.
Gift.

The Star Carol

Lyric by Wihla Hutson
Music by Alfred Burt

Long years ago on a deep winter night,
High in the heav'ns a star shone bright,
While in a manger a wee Infant lay,
Sweetly asleep on a bed of hay.

Jesus, the Lord, was that Baby so small,
Laid down to sleep in a humble stall;
Then came the star and it stood overhead,
Shedding its light 'round His little bed.

Dear Baby Jesus, how tiny Thou art,
I'll make a place for Thee in my heart,
And when the stars in the heavens I see,
Ever and always I think of Thee.

TRO - © Copyright 1954 (Renewed) and 1957 (Renewed) Hollis Music, Inc., New York, NY
International Copyright Secured
All Rights Reserved Including Public Performance For Profit
Used by Permission

The Star of Christmas Morning

Traditional

We saw a light shine out afar,
On Christmas in the morning,
And straight we knew it was Christ's star,
Bright beaming in the morning.

Then did we fall on bended knee,
On Christmas in the morning,
And praised the Lord, who'd let us see
His glory at its dawning.

Copyright © 2006 by HAL LEONARD CORPORATION
International Copyright Secured   All Rights Reserved

The Star Carol
(Canzone d'i zampognari)

English Lyric and Music Adaptation by Peter Seeger
(Based on a Traditional Neapolitan Carol)

'Twas on a night like this,
A little Babe was born;
The shepherds gathered 'round
To guard Him till the dawn.

Above them shown a star,
A star so wond'rous light;
Never since in all these years
Have we seen one half so bright.

Shining so truly, shining so brightly,
Guiding their footsteps from afar.
It led them through the night,
A path to love and brotherhood
By following its light.

Oh, come with us tonight,
And join us on our way;
For we have found that star once more
To greet a better day.

TRO - © Copyright 1952 (Renewed) Folkways Music Publishers, Inc., New York, NY
International Copyright Secured
All Rights Reserved Including Public Performance For Profit
Used by Permission

For though throughout our land
Men search the skies in vain,
Yet turn their glance within their hearts
They would find this star again.

Shining so truly, shining so brightly,
Guiding our footsteps from afar.
It leads us through the night,
A path to love and brotherhood
By following its light.

Still, Still, Still

19th Century Salzburg Melody
Traditional Austrian Text

Still, still, still,
To sleep is now His will.
On Mary's breast He rests in slumber
While we pray in endless number.
Still, still, still,
To sleep is now his will.

Sleep, sleep, sleep,
While we Thy vigil keep.
And angels come from heaven singing
Songs of jubilation bringing
Sleep, sleep, sleep,
While we thy vigil keep.
Sleep, sleep, sleep,
While we thy vigil keep.

Copyright © 2002 by HAL LEONARD CORPORATION
International Copyright Secured   All Rights Reserved

Suzy Snowflake

Words and Music by Sid Tepper and Roy Bennett

Here comes Suzy Snowflake,
Dressed in a snow white gown,
Tap, tap, tappin' at your windowpane
To tell you she's in town.

Here comes Suzy Snowflake,
Soon you will hear her say:
"Come out everyone and play with me;
I haven't long to stay.

If you wanna make a snowman,
I'll help you make one, one, two, three.
If you wanna take a sleigh ride,
The ride's on me."

Here comes Suzy Snowflake,
Look at her tumblin' down,
Bringing joy to every girl and boy;
Suzy's come to town.

Copyright © 1951 by Chappell & Co.
Copyright Renewed
International Copyright Secured   All Rights Reserved

Tennessee Christmas

Words and Music by Amy Grant and Gary Chapman

Come on, weather man,
Give us a forecast snowy white.
Can't you hear the prayers
Of every childlike heart tonight?
Rockies are callin', Denver snow falling.
Somebody said it's four feet deep.
But it doesn't matter, give me the laughter
I'm gonna choose to keep

Refrain:
Another tender Tennessee Christmas.
The only Christmas for me.
Where the love circles around us
Like the gifts around our tree.

Well, I know there's more snow up in Colorado
Than my roof will ever see.
But a tender Tennessee Christmas
Is the only Christmas for me.

Every now and then I get
A wanderin' urge to see.
Maybe California,
Maybe Tinsel Town's for me.
There's a parade there, we'd have it made there.
Bring home a tan for New Year's Eve.
Sure sounds exciting, awfully inviting,
Still I think I'm gonna keep

© 1983 MEADOWGREEN MUSIC COMPANY (ASCAP) and WORD MUSIC, INC.
MEADOWGREEN MUSIC COMPANY Admin. by EMI CMG PUBLISHING
All Rights Reserved   Used by Permission

Refrain

Well, they say in L.A. it's a warm holiday,
It's the only place to be.
But a tender Tennessee Christmas
Is the only Christmas for me.
A tender Tennessee Christmas
Is the only Christmas for me.

That Christmas Feeling

Words and Music by Bennie Benjamin and George Weiss

How I love that Christmas feeling;
How I treasure its friendly glow.
See the way a stranger greets you
Just as though you'd met him Christmases ago.

Christmas helps you to remember
To do what other folks hold dear.
What a blessed place the world would be
If we had that Christmas feeling all year.

Copyright © 1946 by Chappell & Co., Bennie Benjamin Music, Inc. and Abilene Music
Copyright Renewed
All Rights Administered by Chappell & Co.
International Copyright Secured   All Rights Reserved

This Christmas

Words and Music by Donny Hathaway and Nadine McKinnor

Hang all the mistletoe.
I'm gonna get to know you better
This Christmas.
And as we trim the tree,
How much fun it's gonna be together
This Christmas.

Refrain:
The fireside is blazing bright.
We're carolin' through the night
And this Christmas
Will be a very special Christmas for me.

Presents and cards are here.
My world is filled with cheer and you,
This Christmas.
And as I look around
Your eyes outshine the town; they do,
This Christmas.

Refrain

Merry Christmas.
Shake your hand, shake your hand now.
Wish your brother merry Christmas
All over the land now.

Copyright © 1970 by BMG Songs, Kuumba Music Publishing and Crystal Raisin Music
Copyright Renewed
All Rights for Kuumba Music Publishing Administered by BMG Songs
International Copyright Secured   All Rights Reserved

This Is Christmas (Bright, Bright the Holly Berries)

Lyric by Wihla Hutson
Music by Alfred Burt

Bright, bright the holly berries
In the wreath upon the door,
Bright, bright the happy faces
With the thoughts of joys in store.
White, white the snowy meadow
Wrapped in slumber deep and sweet,
White, white the mistletoe
'Neath which two lovers meet.

Refrain:
This is Christmas,
This is Christmas,
This is Christmas time.

Gay, gay the children's voices
Filled with laughter, filled with glee,
Gay, gay the tinseled things
Upon the dark and spicy tree.
Day, day when all mankind
May hear the angel's song again,
Day, day when Christ was born
To bless the sons of men.

Refrain

TRO - © Copyright 1954 (Renewed) and 1957 (Renewed) Hollis Music, Inc., New York, NY
International Copyright Secured
All Rights Reserved Including Public Performance For Profit
Used by Permission

Sing, sing ye heav'nly host
To tell the blessed Savior's birth,
Sing, sing in holy joy,
Ye dwellers all upon the earth.
King, King yet tiny Babe
Come down to us from God above,
King, King of every heart
Which opens wide to love.

Refrain

This One's for the Children

Words and Music by Maurice Starr

There are some people living in this world,
They have no food to eat,
They have no place to go.
But we all are God's children,
We have to learn to love one another.
Just remember they could be us,
Remember, we are all brothers.

Refrain:
I'm not trying to darken up your day,
But help others in need
And show them there's a better way.
This one's for the children,
The children of the world.
This one's for the children,
May God keep them in His throne.

Many people are happy
And many people are sad.
Some people have many things
That others can only wish they had.
So, for the sake of the children,
Show them love's the only way to go,
'Cause they're our tomorrow,
And people, they've got to know.

© 1989 EMI APRIL MUSIC INC. and MAURICE STARR MUSIC
All Rights Controlled and Administered by EMI APRIL MUSIC INC.
All Rights Reserved   International Copyright Secured   Used by Permission

Refrain

This one's for the children,
The children of the world.
This one's for the children,
May God keep them in His throne.
The children of the world.
This one's for the children.

Toyland

Words by Glen MacDonough
Music by Victor Herbert

from the musical *Babes in Toyland*

Toyland! Toyland!
Little girl and boy land,
While you dwell within it,
You are ever happy then.

Childhood's joyland,
Mystic, merry joyland,
Once you pass its borders,
You can never return again.

Copyright © 2002 by HAL LEONARD CORPORATION
International Copyright Secured   All Rights Reserved

Up on the Housetop

Words and Music by B.R. Handy

Up on the housetop reindeer pause,
Out jumps good old Santa Claus;
Down through the chimney with lots of toys,
All for the little ones, Christmas joys.

Refrain:
Ho, ho, ho! Who wouldn't go?
Ho, ho, ho! Who wouldn't go?
Up on the housetop, click, click, click,
Down through the chimney with good Saint Nick.

First comes the stocking of little Nell;
Oh, dear Santa, fill it well.
Give her a dolly that laughs and cries,
One that will open and shut her eyes.

Refrain

Look in the stocking of little Will,
Oh, just see what a glorious fill!
Here is a hammer and lots of tacks,
Whistle and ball and a whip that cracks.

Refrain

Copyright © 2002 by HAL LEONARD CORPORATION
International Copyright Secured   All Rights Reserved

'Twas the Night Before Christmas

Words by Clement Clark Moore
Music by F. Henri Klickman

'Twas the night before Christmas, when all through the house,
Not a creature was stirring, not even a mouse.
The stockings were hung by the chimney with care,
In the hopes that Saint Nicholas soon would be there.
The children were nestled all snug in their beds,
While visions of sugar plums danced through their heads.
And mamma in her 'kerchief, and I in my cap,
Had just settled our brains for a long winter's nap.

When out on the lawn there arose such a clatter,
I sprang from the bed to see what was the matter.
Away to the window I flew like a flash,
Tore open the shutters and threw up the sash.
The moon on the breast of the new-fallen snow
Gave a lustre of midday to objects below.
When, what to my wondering eyes should appear,
But a miniature sleigh and eight tiny reindeer,

With a little old driver, so lively and quick,
I knew in a moment it must be St. Nick.
More rapid than eagles his coursers they came,
And he whistled, and shouted, and called them by name:
"Now, Dasher! Now, Dancer! Now, Prancer and Vixen!
On, Comet! On, Cupid! On, Donner and Blitzen!
To the top of the porch, to the top of the wall!
Now dash away! Dash away! Dash away all!"

Copyright © 2002 by HAL LEONARD CORPORATION
International Copyright Secured   All Rights Reserved

As dry leaves that before the wild hurricane fly,
When they meet with an obstacle, mount to the sky,
So up to the house top the coursers they flew,
With the sleigh full of toys, and St. Nicholas too.
And then, in a twinkling, I heard on the roof
The prancing and pawing of each little hoof.
As I drew in my hand, and was turning around,
Down the chimney St. Nicholas came with a bound.

He was dressed all in fur, from his head to his foot,
And his clothes were all tarnished with ashes and soot;
A bundle of toys he had flung on his back,
And he looked like a peddler just opening his pack.
His eyes, how they twinkled! His dimples, how merry!
His cheeks were like roses, his nose like a cherry!
His droll little mouth was drawn up like a bow,
And the beard of his chin was as white as the snow.

The stump of a pipe he held tight in his teeth,
And the smoke, it encircled his head like a wreath.
He had a broad face and a little round belly
That shook, when he laughed, like a bowl full of jelly.
He was chubby and plump, a right jolly old elf,
And I laughed when I saw him, in spite of myself;
A wink of his eye, and a twist of his head,
Soon gave me to know I had nothing to dread.

He spoke not a word, but went straight to his work,
And filled all the stockings; then turned with a jerk,
And laying his finger aside of his nose,
And giving a nod, up the chimney he rose.
He sprang to his sleigh, to his team gave a whistle,
And away they all fled like the down of a thistle.
But I heard him exclaim, ere he drove out of sight,
"Happy Christmas to all, and to all a good night!"

The Twelve Days of Christmas

Traditional English Carol

On the first day of Christmas,
My true love sent to me
A partridge in a pear tree.

On the second day of Christmas,
My true love sent to me
Two turtle doves
And a partridge in a pear tree.

On the third day of Christmas,
My true love sent to me
Three French hens...
(Etc., counting back to "A partridge in a pear tree")

On the fourth day of Christmas,
My true love sent to me
Four calling birds...

On the fifth day of Christmas,
My true love sent to me
Five golden rings...

On the sixth day of Christmas,
My true love gave to me
Six geese a-laying...

Copyright © 2002 by HAL LEONARD CORPORATION
International Copyright Secured   All Rights Reserved

On the seventh day of Christmas,
My true love gave to me
Seven swans a-swimming...

On the eighth day of Christmas,
My true love gave to me
Eight maids a-milking...

On the ninth day of Christmas,
My true love gave to me
Nine ladies dancing...

On the tenth day of Christmas,
My true love gave to me
Ten lords a-leaping...

On the eleventh day of Christmas,
My true love gave to me
Eleven pipers piping...

On the twelfth day of Christmas,
My true love gave to me
Twelve drummers drumming...

A Virgin Unspotted

Traditional English Carol

A virgin unspotted, the prophet foretold,
Should bring forth a Savior, which we now behold;
To be our Redeemer from death, hell and sin,
Which Adam's transgression had wrapped us in.

Refrain:
Aye, and therefore be merry, set sorrow aside,
Christ Jesus, our Savior, was born on this tide.

Then God sent an angel from Heaven so high,
To certain poor shepherds in fields where they lie,
And bade them no longer in sorrow to stay,
Because that our Savior was born on this day.

Refrain

Then presently after, the shepherds did spy
Vast numbers of angels to stand in the sky;
They joyfully talked and sweetly did sing:
"To God be all glory, our heavenly King."

Refrain

To teach us humility all this was done,
And learn we from thence haughty pride for to shun;
A manger His cradle who came from above,
The great God of mercy, of peace and of love.

Refrain

Copyright © 2006 by HAL LEONARD CORPORATION
International Copyright Secured   All Rights Reserved

We Are Santa's Elves

Music and Lyrics by Johnny Marks

Ho ho ho!
Ho ho ho!
We are Santa's elves.

We are Santa's elves,
Filling Santa's shelves
With a toy for each girl and boy.
Oh, we are Santa's elves.

We work hard all day,
But our work is play.
Dolls we try out,
See if they cry out.
We are Santa's elves.

We've a special job each year.
We don't like to brag.
Christmas Eve we always fill Santa's bag.

Santa knows who's good,
Do the things you should.
And we bet you
He won't forget you.
We are Santa's elves.

Ho ho ho!
Ho ho ho!
We are Santa's elves.
Ho ho!

Copyright © 1964 (Renewed 1992) St. Nicholas Music Inc., 1619 Broadway, New York, New York 10019
All Rights Reserved

We Need a Little Christmas

Music and Lyric by Jerry Herman

from the musical *Mame*

Haul out the holly,
Put up the tree before my
Spirit falls again.
Fill up the stocking,
I may be rushing things, but
Deck the halls again now.

For we need a little Christmas,
Right this very minute,
Candles in the window,
Carols at the spinet.
Yes, we need a little Christmas,
Right this very minute,
It hasn't snowed a single flurry,
But Santa, dear, we're in a hurry.

So climb down the chimney,
Turn on the brightest string of
Lights I've ever seen,
Slice up the fruitcake,
It's time we hung some tinsel
On that evergreen bough.

© 1966 (Renewed) JERRY HERMAN
All Rights Controlled by JERRYCO MUSIC CO.
Exclusive Agent: EDWIN H. MORRIS & COMPANY, A Division of MPL Music Publishing, Inc.
All Rights Reserved

For I've grown a little leaner,
Grown a little colder,
Grown a little sadder,
Grown a little older.
And I need a little angel,
Sitting on my shoulder,
Need a little Christmas now!

For we need a little music,
Need a little laughter,
Need a little singing,
Ringing through the rafter.
And we need a little snappy
"Happy ever after,"
Need a little Christmas now!

We Three Kings of Orient Are

Words and Music by John H. Hopkins, Jr.

We three kings of Orient are;
Bearing gifts we traverse afar,
Field and fountain, moor and mountain,
Following yonder star.

Refrain:
O star of wonder, star of night,
Star with royal beauty bright,
Westward leading, still proceeding,
Guide us to thy perfect light.

Born a King on Bethlehem's plain,
Gold I bring to crown Him again,
King forever, ceasing never
Over us all to reign.

Refrain

Frankincense to offer have I;
Incense owns a Deity nigh;
Prayer and praising, all men raising,
Worship Him, God most high.

Refrain

Copyright © 2002 by HAL LEONARD CORPORATION
International Copyright Secured   All Rights Reserved

Myrrh is mine; its bitter perfume
Breathes a life of gathering gloom;
Sorr'wing, sighing, bleeding, dying,
Sealed in the stone-cold tomb.

Refrain

Glorious now, behold Him arise,
King and God and sacrifice,
Alleluia, alleluia,
Earth to heav'n replies.

Refrain

We Wish You
a Merry Christmas

Traditional English Folksong

We wish you a merry Christmas,
We wish you a merry Christmas,
We wish you a merry Christmas,
And a happy New Year.

Good tiding we bring to you and your kin,
Good tiding for Christmas and a happy New Year.

We all know that Santa's coming,
We all know that Santa's coming,
We all know that Santa's coming,
And soon will be here.

Good tiding we bring to you and your kin,
Good tiding for Christmas and a happy New Year.

We wish you a merry Christmas,
We wish you a merry Christmas,
We wish you a merry Christmas,
And a happy New Year.

Copyright © 2006 by HAL LEONARD CORPORATION
International Copyright Secured   All Rights Reserved

What Are You Doing New Year's Eve?

By Frank Loesser

Maybe it's much too early in the game,
Ah, but I thought I'd ask you just the same,
What are you doing New Year's, New Year's Eve?
Wonder whose arms will hold you good and tight,
When it's exactly twelve o'clock that night,
Welcoming in the new year, New Year's Eve?

Maybe I'm crazy to suppose
I'd ever be the one you chose
Out of a thousand invitations you'll receive.
Ah, but in case I stand one little chance,
Here comes the jackpot question in advance:
What are you doing New Year's, New Year's Eve?

© 1947 (Renewed) FRANK MUSIC CORP.
All Rights Reserved

What Child Is This?

Words by William C. Dix
16th Century English Melody

What child is this, who, laid to rest,
On Mary's lap is sleeping?
Whom angels greet with anthems sweet,
While shepherds watch are keeping?

Refrain:
This, this is Christ the King,
Whom shepherds guard and angels sing:
Haste, haste to bring Him laud,
The Babe, the Son of Mary.

Why lies He in such mean estate
Where ox and ass are feeding?
Good Christian, fear, for sinners here
The silent Word is pleading.

Refrain

So bring Him incense, gold, and myrrh,
Come peasant, king to own Him;
The King of kings salvation brings,
Let loving hearts enthrone Him.

Refrain

Copyright © 2002 by HAL LEONARD CORPORATION
International Copyright Secured   All Rights Reserved

When Santa Claus Gets Your Letter

Music and Lyrics by Johnny Marks

Christmas comes but once a year,
With presents 'round the tree.
When you write to Santa Claus,
Take this tip from me.

When Santa Claus gets your letter,
You know what he will say:
"Have you been good the way you should
On every single day?"

When Santa gets your letter
To ask for Christmas toys,
He'll take a look in his good book
He keeps for girls and boys.

He'll stroke his beard, his eyes will glow,
And at your name he'll peer;
It takes a little time, you know,
To check back one whole year!

When Santa Claus gets your letter,
I really do believe,
You'll head his list, you won't be missed,
By Santa on Christmas Eve.

Copyright © 1950 (Renewed 1978) St. Nicholas Music Inc., 1619 Broadway, New York, New York 10019
All Rights Reserved

Where Are You Christmas?

Words and Music by Will Jennings, James Horner and Mariah Carey

from *Dr. Seuss' How the Grinch Stole Christmas*

Where are you, Christmas?
Why can't I find you?
Why have you gone away?
Where is the laughter
You used to bring me?
Why can't I hear music play?
My world is changing.
I'm rearranging.
Does that mean Christmas changes too?

Where are you, Christmas?
Do you remember
The one you used to know?
I'm not the same one.
See what the time's done.
Is that why you have let me go?

Oh, Christmas is here, everywhere.
Oh, Christmas is here, if you care.
If there is love in your heart and your mind,
You will feel like Christmas all the time.

Copyright © 2000 BLUE SKY RIDER SONGS, UNIVERSAL MUSIC CORP., RYE SONGS, SONGS OF UNIVERSAL, INC.
    and HORNER MUSIC
All Rights for BLUE SKY RIDER SONGS Controlled and Administered by IRVING MUSIC, INC.
All Rights for RYE SONGS Controlled and Administered by UNIVERSAL MUSIC CORP.
All Rights Reserved   Used by Permission

I feel you, Christmas,
I know I found you.
You never fade away.
Oh, the joy of Christmas
Stays here inside us,
Fills each and every heart with love.

Where are you, Christmas?
Fill your heart with love.

While Shepherds Watched Their Flocks

Words by Nahum Tate
Music by George Frideric Handel

While shepherds watched their flocks by night,
All seated on the ground,
The angel of the Lord came down,
And glory shone around.

"Fear not," said he, for mighty dread
Had seized their troubled mind.
"Glad tidings of great joy I bring
To you and all mankind.

"To you in David's town this day
Is born of David's line
A Savior, who is Christ the Lord,
And this shall be the sign.

"The heav'nly babe you there shall find
To human view displayed,
All meanly wrapped in swathing bands
And in a manger laid."

Thus spoke the seraph, and forthwith
Appeared a shining throng
Of angels praising God on high,
Who thus addressed their song:

"All glory be to God on high,
And on the earth be peace;
Goodwill henceforth from heav'n to earth
Begin and never cease!"

Copyright © 2002 by HAL LEONARD CORPORATION
International Copyright Secured   All Rights Reserved

The White World of Winter

Words by Mitchell Parish
Music by Hoagy Carmichael

In this wonderful white world of winter,
Darling, we'll have a wonderful time;
First, we'll ride side by side through the hinter
And rondelay to the sleighbell's merrie chime;
Then we'll ski fancy free down the mountains
And take those chances all silly people do.
If there's ever a moment you are freezin',
Just a little squeezin' could be mighty pleasin',
In this wonderful white world of winter,
I'm fallin' head over heels over you.

In this wonderful white world of winter,
Darling, we'll have a wonderful time;
If we prayed it would snow all this winter,
I ask ya, is that a terr'ble horr'ble crime?
I can't wait till we skate on Lake Happy
And sup a hot buttered cup in the afterglow.
If there's ever a moment you're not laughin',
Maybe a toboggan split your little noggin'.
In this wonderful white world of winter,
I'm thinkin' you are the sweetest one I know.

Copyright © 1965 by Songs Of Peer, Ltd. and Cromwell Music, Inc., New York, NY
Copyright Renewed
International Copyright Secured   All Rights Reserved

Why Christmas

Words and Music by Wanya Morris

Every day at this time of year
I wonder time and time again
Why are kids suffering?
All of the tears 'cause being caught in the crossfire
Somebody tell me why.
As the joyous day comes along,
The eldest feel there's something wrong.
He's lookin' for Mom but she's not there.
Kids are looking for reindeer in the air.

Refrain:
She messed up again. Why?
My brother and my sister, they ain't got no toys.
What am I supposed to do
When growing up for me wasn't joy?
It's gonna be a why Christmas.
It's gonna be, it's gonna be a,
A why Christmas.

No one was there but Grandma and her friends;
A time of heartache is setting in.
There's nothin' I can do
Just sit and feel pain run through.
I often wished they were never born.
The thought of them not having no toys.
Their little hearts were torn.
I was young and I cried as well.
I didn't have a job,
But I prayed to the Lord that there'd be better days.
Yes, he gave me a reason to live, he gave me a sign.
But I still think to that day when

Refrain

Copyright © 1993 by Squirt Shot Publishing and Ensign Music LLC
International Copyright Secured   All Rights Reserved

You're All I Want for Christmas

Words and Music by Glen Moore and Seger Ellis

When Santa comes around at Christmas time
And leaves a lot of cheer at every door,
If he would only grant the wish in my heart
I would never ask for more.

You're all I want for Christmas,
All I want my whole life through.
Each day is just like Christmas
Any time that I'm with you.

You're all I want for Christmas,
And if all my dreams come true,
Then I'll awake on Christmas morning
And find my stocking filled with you.

Copyright © 1948 SONGS OF UNIVERSAL, INC.
Copyright Renewed
All Rights Reserved   Used by Permission

Wonderful Christmastime

Words and Music by Paul McCartney

The mood is right, the spirit's up,
We're here tonight and that's enough.
Simply having a wonderful Christmastime.
Simply having a wonderful Christmastime.

The party's on, the feeling's here
That only comes this time of year.
Simply having a wonderful Christmastime.
Simply having a wonderful Christmastime.

The choir of children sing their song.
Ding dong, ding dong.
Ding, dong, ding.
Ooh, ooh.
Do do do do do do do.

We're simply having a wonderful Christmastime.
Simply having a wonderful Christmastime.

The word is out about the town,
To lift a glass, oh, don't look down.
Simply having a wonderful Christmastime.
Simply having a wonderful Christmastime.

© 1979 MPL COMMUNICATIONS LTD.
Administered by MPL COMMUNICATIONS, INC.
All Rights Reserved

The choir of children sing their song.
(They practiced all year long.)
Ding dong, ding dong, ding dong,
Ding dong, ding dong, ding dong,
Dong, dong, dong, dong.

The party's on, the spirit's up.
We're here tonight and that's enough.
Simply having a wonderful Christmastime.
We're simply having a wonderful Christmastime.

You Don't Have to Be Alone

Words and Music by Veit Renn, Joshua Chasez and David Nicoll

I don't know when we fell apart.
The love that we had was like a work of art.
I used to see heaven in your eyes.
Now angels are falling from your skies.
Things we said were so wrong,
And I haven't held you for so long.
My foolish pride turns me inside.
Why did we tell all those lies?
You can reach for the phone.
You don't have to be alone.

Refrain:
Outside the winter seems so cold.
Your heart has frozen like the snow.
And there's no one home
To keep you safe and warm.
Your eyes are red because you cried.
You fell asleep by the fireside.
But there's one thing you should know;
On this Christmas, baby,
You don't have to be alone.

Copyright © 2001 by Chasez Music and Galactic Nicoll Music
All Rights Administered by Zomba Enterprises, Inc.
International Copyright Secured   All Rights Reserved

And I had only one wish on my list.
For me, you would be the perfect girl.
There's nothing colder than an empty home.
And hotter days were never meant to be alone.
The smiles we gave when our hearts were safe
By each other's love and warmth.
That subsided now, no happiness around.
If I can only find a way to your heart.

Refrain

You don't have to be alone.
You don't have to be all alone at home.
You don't have to be alone.
You don't have to be alone.

Refrain

The
PAPERBACK LYRIC COLLECTION
from  HAL•LEONARD®

CHRISTMAS
Includes: All I Want for Christmas Is You • Auld Lang Syne • Away in a Manger • Baby, It's Cold Outside • Happy Xmas (War Is Over) • Hark! The Herald Angels Sing • Jingle-Bell Rock • Silver Bells • and more.
00240273 ....$7.95

THE 1950s
Timeless classics include: All Shook Up • At the Hop • Blue Suede Shoes • Blueberry Hill • Donna • Fever • Jambalaya (On the Bayou) • Misty • Peggy Sue • Rock Around the Clock • Splish Splash • Unchained Melody • Walkin' After Midnight • and more.
00240274 ....$7.95

THE 1960s
Classics include: All You Need Is Love • Beyond the Sea • California Dreamin' • Downtown • Hey Jude • It's My Party • Leaving on a Jet Plane • Louie, Louie • Respect • Stand by Me • Twist and Shout • more.
00240275 ....$7.95

THE 1970s
Favorites include: American Pie • Anticipation • Cat's in the Cradle • (They Long to Be) Close to You • Dust in the Wind • Fire and Rain • I Am Woman • Imagine • Reunited • Y.M.C.A. • You're So Vain • Your Song • and more.
00240276 ....$7.95

Visit Hal Leonard online at
www.halleonard.com

THE 1980s
Hits include: Another One Bites the Dust • Call Me • Candle in the Wind • Crazy Little Thing Called Love • 867-5309/Jenny • Every Breath You Take • Fast Car • Footloose • Hurts So Good • Legs • Longer • Missing You • and more.
00240277 ....$7.95

THE 1990s
Collection includes: All I Wanna Do • Beauty and the Beast • Black Velvet • Closer to Free • Come to My Window • Fields of Gold • Iris • More Than Words • Smells like Teen Spirit • Smooth • Tears in Heaven • Walking in Memphis • and more.
00240278 ....$7.95

THE 2000s
Today's hits, including: Accidentally in Love • Behind These Hazel Eyes • Beverly Hills • Breathe (2 AM) • Clocks • Drops of Jupiter (Tell Me) • The Middle • Mr. Brightside • 100 Years • Redneck Woman • You Raise Me Up • and more.
00240279 ....$7.95

Prices, contents and availability are subject to change without notice.
Some products may not be available outside the U.S.A.

FOR MORE INFORMATION, SEE YOUR LOCAL MUSIC DEALER, OR WRITE TO:

HAL•LEONARD®
CORPORATION
7777 W. BLUEMOUND RD. P.O. BOX 13819 MILWAUKEE, WI 53213